ONE OF OUR OWN

ONE OF OUR OWN

The Remarkable Story of Battle of Britain
Pilot Squadron Leader Victor Ekins MBE DFC

DAVID DUKER

AIR WORLD

AIR WORLD

ONE OF OUR OWN
The Remarkable Story of Battle of Britain Pilot
Squadron Leader Victor Ekins MBE DFC

First published in Great Britain in 2023 by
Air World
An imprint of
Pen & Sword Books Ltd
Yorkshire – Philadelphia

ISBN: 978 1 39905 067 8

Typeset by SJmagic DESIGN SERVICES, India.
Printed and bound in the UK by CPI Group (UK) Ltd.

Pen & Sword Books Ltd incorporates the imprints of Pen & Sword Archaeology, Air World Books, Atlas, Aviation, Battleground, Discovery, Family History, History, Maritime, Military, After the Battle, Naval, Politics, Social History, Transport, True Crime, Claymore Press, Frontline Books, Praetorian Press, Seaforth Publishing and White Owl

For a complete list of Pen & Sword titles please contact:

PEN & SWORD BOOKS LTD
George House, Units 12 & 13, Beevor Street, Off Pontefract Road, Barnsley, South Yorkshire, S71 1HN, England
Website: www.pen-and-sword.co.uk

or

PEN AND SWORD BOOKS,
1950 Lawrence Road, Havertown, PA 19083, USA
E-mail: uspen-and-sword@casematepublishers.com
Website: www.penandswordbooks.com

Contents

Acknowledgements

This fascinating project would not have been possible without the support of a dedicated network of people and I would like to take the opportunity to acknowledge their contribution.

Firstly, I would like to give thanks to the Ekins family. They have been so supportive throughout the entire project and the many hours that we have spent together discussing Victor, Kim and so much more has been time that I shall never forget. A project like this needs openness, honesty, trust and commitment to have any chance of success and this has been ever present since day one. It has allowed us the privilege of travelling back in time and unlocking more than eighty years of untold stories that have brought the achievements and personality of this great man to life. Quite simply, this book would not exist without the unequivocal support of Victor's two sons, Anthony and Paul Ekins. Thank you chaps.

Whilst on the subject of family, next I have to acknowledge the almost unimaginable contribution made to this book by my incredible mother, Chris Duker. Her dedication to the project has been invaluable. Not only did she spend almost three months transcribing the 80,000 words from Victor's diaries that form the foundation of what you are about to read but she has been there every step of the way as we undertook hundreds of hours of research. To have her so involved has been a dream to me personally and we have spent many a happy hour together travelling back in time and learning all about a very special person from this unique era. It has given us the opportunity to create some cherished memories of working together that will last a lifetime. Thank you my dear.

I also have to share my gratitude for my loving and supportive family. This has been a goliath project that couldn't have happened without my wife, Emma, and two daughters, Evie and Emily. Those who know me understand that family comes first and the space that they have afforded me to write and research without question has been vital. I have always endeavoured to find a balance but at no stage have I ever felt anything other than their love and support.

A book of this nature has taken many hundreds of hours of research and this has been made all the more possible with the support, encouragement and assistance of Dave Brocklehurst MBE from the Kent Battle of Britain Museum. Dave is a leading expert on the subject of the battle and, from the early stages of trying to track down the Ekins family to the sometimes-daunting challenges of research, he has always been there with his expert knowledge and guidance.

I would also like to acknowledge the time spent with Victor's goddaughter, Marion Bird, who was able to share her beautifully unique perspective of time spent with 'Vic'. Despite the passing of time, Marion still lovingly carries with her a picture of her godfather, and that affection infused every sentence of the conversations we had. This was a man who was held in incredibly high esteem by all who knew him.

One of the real challenges of writing *One of Our Own* was illuminating the years that Victor spent commanding 19 Squadron. We had access to his diaries, alongside a wealth of photographs taken from the era but desperately needed to join the dots. In finding Roger Llywelyn Henderson we probably found the only person on the planet who could answer the many questions that we had. It was fascinating listening to Roger, a man who personally knew many of the pilots in question, and learn about Victor's time as a squadron leader. I cannot mention Roger's involvement without also acknowledging the role of Dilip Sarkar MBE, who kindly introduced us. Dilip is another leading expert on the subject of the Battle of Britain who has been incredibly supportive throughout.

Finally, for their support and input I would like to thank my father, Rob Duker, Linda Duffield from the Kenley Revival, Liz Davies from the St Neots Museum, David Stanbridge, Jonny Cracknell, Russ Edgar and Kirsty Goddard.

Everybody mentioned has been vital in creating what you are about to read and I will be forever grateful to you all.

Author's Notes

Writing *One of Our Own* has quite simply been the privilege of a lifetime. I hold the generation who overcame the huge challenge of the Second World War in the highest regard and to be able to immerse myself in the story of one man's journey has been an honour. Victor Ekins was an incredibly special person who, like so many, gave his all to repel the dark cloud of war that had fallen over the world. His modest and understated nature would have baulked at such a statement but the fact is we are talking about a man who had a natural intuition when it comes to the human spirit. Victor could make connections with ease but his almost imperceptible skill was nurturing a connection that struck a deeper chord. Whether it was his engaging personality, his obvious strength of character or the fact that he genuinely wanted the best for those lucky enough to make his acquaintance, he was a man tailor-made for leadership. His diligence in keeping five years' worth of wartime diaries has seen him become a spiritual guide to this project and has allowed us to illuminate an otherwise untold story of human endeavour. True to form, Victor himself has led the way and I have been in the rather wonderful position of following his lead.

This is the story of Victor's war. The narrative of the book is his account. If an event or personality was pertinent enough for him to write about in his diary, then I have endeavoured to reflect that in this book. I wanted to do justice to those who made an impression on his life. We have been in the fortunate position of being able to access his pilot's logbook, the Operational Record Book for every day that he served with a front-line squadron and his own personal diaries. The entries that he made during those tumultuous years have given us a fascinating and personal insight into Victor's world. It is not the sort of diary that could be published as it is, with each entry being short, sharp and extremely matter of fact. Victor dedicated himself to keeping a record of squadron life, which can be shown by the fact that he would regularly draft somebody in to carry on if he was absent on leave but the diary was never intended to be expressive or creative. Like the man himself, the document that had laid unopened for over eighty years was direct and to the point. The real skill when working with the diaries was to never underestimate the depth of a short statement and, in some cases, a single word. Yet, despite the practical nature of his writing, it is a document full of feeling and it has been my privilege to take the time to get in tune with it during our research.

The project has been a true team effort. Working with Anthony and Paul Ekins over the last few years has been such a privilege and their openness, trust and enthusiasm for telling their father's story has been absolutely vital to its success. Quite simply, this book is for them. It's a modest account of the life of a member of the Ekins family, a local hero and one of this nation's 'Few'. Of a young man that could be counted upon when his nation and indeed the free world needed him the most. Yes, Victor Ekins was a Battle of Britain pilot but more importantly what has emerged is the story of a good man.

After in-depth conversations with Victor's family and close acquaintances it soon became apparent that, like so many of their generation, neither he nor Kim chose to speak about their wartime experiences. They gave up six of their youthful years in service of their country and, once their duty was complete, very much closed that chapter of their life. I have lived in Victor's home town of St Neots my entire life and have also held a lifelong passion for the Battle of Britain but a measure of the modesty can be seen by the fact that I had never heard about his wartime achievements. This whole project began by the chance discovery of a document online, my connection to the wonderful Kent Battle of Britain Museum and the sheer fact that Anthony and Judith Ekins saw fit to let a complete stranger into their house after I had rather boldly knocked on their door to introduce myself. After explaining my background and sharing my view that Victor should be recognised locally, perhaps with a blue plaque, Anthony invited me into his garage as he had a few items of his father's that 'may be of interest'. What he showed me stopped me in my tracks. After opening a very modest and unassuming storage box, there, set out in front of me was the most wonderful and complete collection of photographs and memorabilia that one could wish to see. It was a remarkable catalogue of Victor's experiences and, to top it off, it was complemented by his wartime diaries. It was obvious from the outset that a personal and unique story was just sitting there, waiting to be told.

What emerged was a story of duty, unity, courage and resilience. A story of a young man who was subjected to the extremes of the Battle of Britain and, despite daunting odds, managed not only to survive the ordeal but would go through the most intense period of personal progress of his entire life. Victor would experience the agony of being part of a squadron that was absolutely decimated, as time and again friends and colleagues lost their lives in pursuit of freedom. His time spent with 111 Squadron would stay with him forever but, despite the relentless demands of life-or-death combat, Victor's stoicism and positive demeanour proved to be a tonic to those around him. The natural shoots of leadership were evident from the very beginning and would lead him on a journey that culminated in being given command of a squadron of his own. He revelled in the brotherhood of squadron life, nurturing bonds that would last a lifetime and were impossible to replicate unless you had experienced those epic days serving with Fighter Command during the Second World War.

One of Our Own is a story packed full of action, loss and duty – but also love. The unavoidable thread that runs through the book is the relationship that he formed with his beloved Kim, who served as a 'plotter' with the Women's Auxiliary Air Force (WAAF). Their wartime stories entwined into a beautiful narrative that would play out to the soundtrack of air raid sirens and exploding bombs. It would go on to last a lifetime.

It is my pleasure to share with you the story of Squadron Leader Victor Ekins MBE DFC – 'One of Our Own'.

1

The Early Years

As the storm clouds of the First World War gathered over Europe, Victor Howard Ekins was born on 16 April 1914, in the back bedroom of 28 New Street, St Neots. He joined a family with a very strong standing in this thriving and picturesque market town, where community and agriculture were the heartbeat of everyday life. His father, Sydney Victor Ekins, was one of five children born to Henry and Anne. Described as being a real 'gentleman', Sydney was a modest, hard-working man who built a successful land agency practice and livestock auction that put the Ekins family in the centre of their local community.

Victor's mother, Grace Maude Gilbert, was one of three children, born to Alfred and Frances. Alfred was a wine and spirit merchant who had brought his young family up in the Wheatsheaf Pub in Eaton Socon, before becoming the Landlord at the Wrestlers Inn, also in New Street. Known to everyone as 'Maude', her young life would have also seen her at the heart of this thriving community. Sydney

Sydney Victor Ekins.

and Maude had married in 1913 and their family was complete when Victor's beloved younger sister, Cynthia, was born in 1918.

For the Ekins family, life was a very social affair. Sydney was running a livestock auction that would go on to be one of the largest

Maude, Victor and Cynthia Ekins.

in East Anglia with over a thousand pigs, eighty cattle and fifty sheep being sold each week. Victor was to grow up in an environment where human interaction and connection were the norm as farmers from across the county would descend upon St Neots to do business at the auction yard and catch up at what became their weekly local meeting place. The noises, smells, hustle and bustle of life at the livestock auction would have been etched into Victor's young mind as it was situated adjacent to the Ekins family home.

He was gaining an education in life, observing both wealthy landowners and drovers alike. Despite the obvious difference in their comparative classes, Victor realised that many of the drovers were good people. At an early age he began to formulate the view that people should be judged by their actions and the strength of their character, not their social standing. Along with these interpersonal skills, there were also many very practical skills that needed to be acquired, not least, how to catch a pig. Victor soon realised that it was useless trying to chase pigs down in a conventional way but the trick with these most elusive of opponents was to hold your nerve and wait until it ran past. He would then run his hand down its side and catch it by the back leg. This skill sounds easy but took a lot of practise and was to be passed down the generations of the Ekins family.

These early lessons and opportunities for intense social observation were beginning to forge a young man of strength and independence. Victor was acquiring a keen sense of what he deemed as 'just' in this world and due to his developing strength of character he wasn't afraid to stand up for what he thought was right. In the Ekins family home this manifested itself primarily through his love for his sister, Cynthia. Their mother had a very selfish view of what it means to parent a child, and often Cynthia would be expected to be at her beck and call. Victor would see his sister treated as a servant, something that would continue throughout her life, and it awakened a strong and undeniable protective streak within him along with an intense

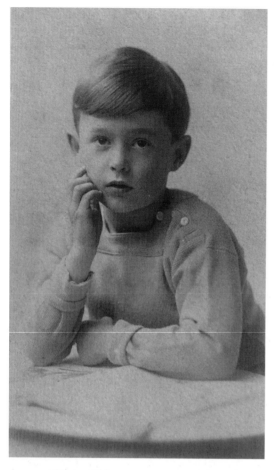

A young Victor Ekins.

feeling of defiance when it came to his relationship with his mother. These traits of protection and defiance would become a strong ally during the arduous wartime years ahead.

Despite there being no records to confirm it, in later years Victor would proudly claim that as a young boy he had attended 'Eton'. He would then pause momentarily before revealing that the 'Eton' in question was in fact Eaton Socon School, much to his amusement. At the age of 7, it was decided that he would leave the Ekins family home and head off to boarding school. He attended the Glebe House Preparatory School in Hunstanton before completing the remainder of his school years at Bishop's Stortford College.

During this time, the independence within Victor grew exponentially. These years strengthened his resolve as he undertook the quite daunting task of navigating through schooling without the direct support of his family. He was on his own. Attending boarding school taught Victor many valuable but hard-earned lessons. He learnt very quickly that to survive and then ultimately thrive in this kind of school environment he would have to keep his emotions within.

Any weakness shown would have been recognised by others and exploited, so Victor soon became quite self-contained. He certainly wasn't withdrawn but he wasn't an extrovert either. Whether he was feeling jubilant or despondent, he developed the ability to keep it in check and carry on as normal. Not only was he learning about himself and his own mindset but he was also learning vast amounts about interpersonal relationships with his peers. Make no mistake, Victor Ekins was a people's person, forging strong friendships and beginning to understand the importance of strong leadership. He had a natural intuition for those around him, being able to look somebody straight in the eye and somehow connect to their soul.

Real personal progress was being made that was no more apparent than within the sporting arena. Victor enjoyed all sports but played rugby to a high standard and excelled at water sport. His love for water would last his entire life. In the December 1931 issue of the *Stortfordian* he was described as an 'outstanding' member of the water polo team, his chief assets being his 'ball control and shooting'.

At the age of 18, and having successfully completed his education, Victor returned to St Neots and joined the family business. He worked hard to

Victor was a keen sportsman. Here he is photographed at 28 New Street about to enjoy a game of tennis.

gain a qualification and soon became a member of the Chartered Auctioneers and Estate Agents Institute, sitting his exams in London and staying at the Bonington Hotel. Life continued in St Neots for a few years but something was stirring within Victor. Partly the natural call to adventure of a young man but also a restlessness and unease around his relationship with his mother. He needed his own space and a job offer through his friend Hilton Morris proved to be the opportunity that he was looking for.

In 1937 Victor joined the Land Settlement Association (LSA) and moved to Birdham, near Chichester in Sussex, to start his new career. The LSA was a government scheme formed in 1934 with the purpose of resettling unemployed workers from depressed industrial areas, mainly from the north-east of England and Wales. The idea was to give them a second chance at life and an opportunity to run a small holding of approximately 5 acres. This land would include livestock and a newly built house, with the new tenant given training

Victor, with pipe in mouth, driving a speed boat with friends.

on how to manage it successfully. It was a job absolutely tailor-made for Victor. Combining his natural leadership abilities and knowledge of agriculture with his deep respect for good people, regardless of their social standing, his job was to assist their move to the small settlements and bring them up to speed with regard to the practical and business skills needed for such an undertaking. Another massive advantage to the move was the positive relationship that he forged with his landlady, Mrs Haskins. She became a constant for Victor throughout the following years and their friendship would carry on long after the war. Life had settled and he threw himself into his work, but both he and the whole country had a keen and necessary eye on the developments that were taking place in Europe.

2

Storm Clouds

Once again, the storm clouds of war were gathering. A mere twenty-one years after the end of a conflict that had decimated so many of the lives of his parents' generation, Germany was again becoming the aggressor of Europe. A young corporal who had served in the trenches of the First World War, Adolf Hitler, had made an astonishing rise to power and was determined to right the many perceived wrongs of the Treaty of Versailles. His desire to reunite German speakers and gain 'living space' for his people had manifested into a very aggressive foreign policy and, as yet, the rest of Europe was loath to oppose him. Despite Germany reoccupying the Rhineland, forming an 'Anschluss' with Austria and forcing Czechoslovakia to surrender the Sudetenland, an allied policy of appeasement was the order of the day.

Despite this policy, the obvious threat posed by the rapidly growing German armed forces could not be ignored. Plans were put in place for Britain to speed up its own rearmament and this included a real push for personnel to join the Royal Air Force Volunteer Reserve, which had been formed in 1936. The Volunteer Reserve (VR) was an organisation designed for a rapid expansion of numbers that would complement the already existing Auxiliary Air Force (the flying equivalent to the Territorial Army) and the 'regular' members of the RAF. This rapid expansion meant that the VR would accept members from all walks of life and backgrounds, giving ordinary folk the opportunity to learn the art of flying, something that otherwise would have been unattainable due to the expense. It was mostly made up of either professionals or people who already had a steady job and wouldn't have to rely on the VR as their main source of income. Successful applicants would continue to work their normal week, learn to fly at weekends and expect to be called up should the worst happen.

There was also a bigger question for the young men of this generation who could by now see the prospect of war looming large on the horizon. If it did happen, what role did they want to play in it? For those who had the foresight to do so, this was a point well worth considering. The experiences of Sydney Ekins' generation, who had seen the horrors of trench warfare, knew how personal fighting as an infantryman was. Living among the dirt and looking into the eyes of the person whose life you are about to take was a brutal undertaking. Joining the RAF meant a different experience altogether. It was no less dangerous but warfare among the clouds still had an air of chivalry attached to it as airmen would duel to shoot down the opposing *aircraft* and not necessarily its pilot. There was also the promise of a hot meal and a few pints at the local pub should they be lucky enough to have survived another day of operations.

Whether it was the call to adventure and the promise of learning a skill that would see him frolicking among the clouds at 20,000ft or simply the prospect of entering the war on his own terms, Victor's mind was made up. Around the time when Britain's Prime Minister, Neville Chamberlain, returned from Munich following crunch talks with Hitler proclaiming 'Peace in our time', Victor Ekins applied to join the RAF Volunteer Reserve. After negotiating the interview successfully, which was no easy task, and progressing past the medical, he was formally accepted into the Royal Air Force VR (RAFVR) as a sergeant pilot under training on 16 March 1939. Posted to 16 Elementary and Reserve Flying Training School at Shoreham, he would commence weekend flying in the De Havilland Tiger Moth, making the hour-long journey from Mrs Haskins' house in Chichester each week.

On his arrival at Shoreham, it was made very clear to all trainees that just because it was easier than ever before to join the Royal Air Force with the VR, it was also damned easy to get out of. Only the best would suffice as the search for men and not boys began in earnest. If the pilots didn't meet the grade with either their flying, ground work or general attitude then the instructors wouldn't think twice about handing out the dreaded 'bowler hats'. This was an RAF term used when your services were no longer required for pilot training and you had to return to civvy street. Needless to say, the very thought struck fear into each and every person on the course. Victor was by now 25 years old, which made him considerably older and, in theory, more mature than most of his counterparts but the going would be tough and the workload immense.

On 21 March Victor walked out onto the airfield for the first time in his flying kit to be confronted by the wonderful sights, sounds and smells of a working airbase lined with Tiger Moths. He had joined a select group of young men with shared interests all striving towards a common goal. The atmosphere was intoxicating. A quick glance at the flying roster for the day and it soon became clear that Victor's instructor would be Flying Officer Grieve and they would be flying Tiger Moth K4256. After being shown the basics of how to strap yourself into the seat of this biplane, they were under way and rumbling across the grass airfield. As the aircraft gained speed, the tail lifted and before long they were airborne, revealing the beautiful scene below as the Tiger Moth gained height. The freedom of flight and sense of doing something new and exciting was all encompassing. After a few minutes had passed the real work began as Victor was asked to carefully place his hands on the controls and feet on the rudder bar, and gently follow his instructor's movements as he was shown the basics of flight. This first, unforgettable trip lasted for half an hour as he was introduced to 'straight and level flight' and 'taxying and handling of the engine'.

So began an intense but extremely exciting period of Victor's life where he worked for the LSA during the week, knowing that in theory he'd be airborne once again within a matter of days. His next opportunity came on 23 March as Flying Officer Townsend introduced him to the art of stalls, climbs and turns, but he then had to wait almost a month before he could take to the skies again. All it took was a weekend of bad weather and the fledgling pilots would have to wait another week. This was the very real drawback to weekend flying. It proved so hard to build momentum as you were learning a very complicated skill in a very short and extremely intense period of time. You would have a great few days of training and then just as you were getting into your stride, you'd find yourself back at work.

Nevertheless, having covered taking off into the wind, turns, approaches and landing, Victor was making good progress. He was a hard-working and diligent young man who applied himself fully to the task in hand. On 6 June, after twelve hours and thirty-five minutes of dual flight, he took off once again, this time flying with Pilot Officer Russell and successfully completed three 'circuits'. After thirty-five minutes he was asked to taxi back to the flight line, whereby his instructor jumped out of the Tiger Moth, tightened the straps in the aircraft and climbed onto the wing to talk to his student. This was the moment that all aspiring pilots dreamed off and one that represented a huge hurdle that needed to be overcome – Victor was about to go solo.

There was really nothing for it but to open the throttle, control the swing as the Tiger Moth picked up speed and lift purposely off the ground. Victor Ekins was sitting alone in an aircraft and he was airborne – it was a huge moment. He did a single circuit of the airfield, lined up his aircraft for landing and sunk back down to earth with a gratifying thud. The flight had lasted less than ten minutes but it was a moment that no one could ever take away from him – he was a pilot. Granted there was a long way to go before he could gain his 'wings' and he knew full well that only his best would be good enough but he had successfully gone solo. The sky was the limit and Victor was in his element.

Maintaining the diversity of his routine and the intensity of the path that he had chosen, the summer months of 1939 were full of blissful flying in the open cockpits of the Tiger Moth – pure aviation. Halcyon days as the pilots of 16 E&RFTS began practising aerobatics in the sun-drenched skies of West Sussex. His time at Shoreham came to an end on 27 August after he had successfully completed forty-eight hours and forty minutes of flying, of which twenty-three hours were solo. Victor's confidence and prowess were growing steadily but news was about to break that changed everything.

On 1 September 1939 Germany, along with their then ally Russia, invaded Poland. It was another aggressive roll of the dice for Hitler as he anticipated yet more appeasement from his European counterparts but the time had come to make a stand. On 3 September 1939 Britain declared war on Germany. Victor received his 'call up' papers and, after packing up his belongings and saying his farewells to Mrs Haskins and his colleagues at the LSA, a new life beckoned as he began full-time service with the Royal Air Force.

He was briefly posted to 3 Initial Training Wing (ITW) at Hastings as the RAF sorted through and placed the large numbers of RAF personnel that had so recently been called up. Staying at Marine Court, a large building on the seafront at St Leonards-on-Sea, Victor spent three gloomy weeks marching up and down the promenade learning the intricacies of arms drill, service discipline and command. It was deemed necessary for pilots of the VR who had been weekend flying in the relatively relaxed flying club atmosphere to learn about the more structured way of life in the Royal Air Force, much to the annoyance of the trainees. It was also here that Victor received his service uniform and flying kit in preparation for the next stage of his journey, which would see him join 4 Elementary Flying Training School at Brough.

The challenge now was to put the last few months on the ground behind him and take to the skies once again. His first flight at Brough took place on 7 November 1939 flying a Blackburn B2 biplane under the instruction of Flight Lieutenant Ball. This was quite a rare aircraft as pilot and instructor would sit side by side in an open cockpit. Victor settled very quickly back into his flight training and, despite the frenetic pace and upheaval of the previous few months, went solo in this new type of aircraft only two days later. There was a new intensity to proceedings that he had yet to experience as his country and indeed the free world rapidly readied itself for war. Victor was now benefiting greatly from full-time training and was able to take to the skies thirty-eight times by the end of November, including his first experience of a cross-country navigation flight.

The solid foundation of training that he'd received at Shoreham was clearly evident to his instructors as they began to demand more and more from their student. Despite the challenging weather and flying conditions of that winter, Victor took his 'ab initio' flying test on 10 January 1940 with his examiner for the day, Flight Sergeant Whitwell. Having now accumulated well over 100 hours of flight he passed with flying colours, being assessed as 'above average'. In the Royal Air Force's most understated way of assessing pilots, 'above average' was only bettered by 'exceptional'.

Every hour of flight, every challenging moment, every off day, every cross-country success were all vital experiences for a young man destined for war. He shared these experiences along with precious memories of flight with the other members of the course. It was a tantalising glimpse into the bond between airmen, who knew and respected the very real dangers of the profession that they had undertaken. In a matter of months, fate would dictate that the only thing keeping the might of the Luftwaffe at bay would be these very same brave young souls.

As Europe held its breath in the inertia of the 'Phoney War', pensively awaiting Hitler's next move, Victor was posted to No. 8 Flying Training School (FTS) at Montrose to complete the next stage of his training. He would now be flying the Miles Master – an advanced monoplane trainer with an enclosed cockpit and retractable

Still yet to receive his pilot 'wings', Victor stands second from right with other RAF recruits.

undercarriage. The Master was vastly superior in performance to anything that Victor had previously flown and was a great stepping stone for a fledgling fighter pilot who was destined for the might and power of the Spitfire or Hurricane. This was the advanced stage of his training and successful completion of the course at Montrose meant one thing – being issued with his pilot's 'wings'. Despite currently wearing the blue uniform of the RAF, it looked naked without that cherished and elusive badge sewn onto its chest. This was the dream. To be a fully qualified, front-line pilot of the Royal Air Force destined for a posting to Fighter Command and the prospect of flying fighters.

Victor took his first flight in the Master on 11 March 1940 and went solo in the aircraft only five days later. The intensity of ground exams and flight training was immense as he began to pull together the last twelve months' worth of experience flying with the RAF. One day could see him performing climbing turns, loops, rolls and aerobatics, the next air navigation and cross-country. He worked under the experienced tuition of Pilot Officer Price and by the end of April had notched up over 140 hours of flight. On 8 May 1940 Victor began the process of examinations that would make up his 'wings' test, being examined by Squadron Leader Louden. Just two days later German forces swept into France, Belgium and the Low Countries as Hitler's Blitzkrieg campaign on mainland Europe raged. It was to be a lightning-paced six weeks of battle that would end in the evacuation at Dunkirk and the fall of Europe to Nazi Germany. The Hurricane squadrons that had been sent to France to support the Allies would return wearied, and in need of replacement pilots but with a greater understanding of their enemy and how to overcome them.

For Victor, timing was everything. Whether it was a conscious decision or not, beginning his training when he did allowed him time and space to explore flight fully. On 28 June 1940 he successfully passed No. 8 FTS and was able to proudly display the Royal Air Force 'wings' above the breast pocket of his uniform. It truly was a day to remember. He was a fully qualified pilot but now an even more important task beckoned – becoming a fully qualified pilot ready for war, and time was of the essence. There really was no let up.

On 1 July 1940 Victor started training at No. 7 Operational Training Unit (OTU) at Hawarden. Here he would learn and develop the skills to serve the RAF operationally. Flying with Sergeant Pilkington, he took to the skies in a Fairey Battle as the last stage before his conversion to fighters. The Battle was pretty much already obsolete as a front-line aircraft but was powered by the Rolls-Royce Merlin engine that also powered both the Supermarine Spitfire and Hawker Hurricane, and offered a great way to prepare pilots for this huge increase in performance. The following day Victor sat at the

Victor photographed at RAF Montrose on the day of receiving his 'wings'.

controls of a Hurricane for the first time. Feeling the vibrations of the aircraft under his seat and looking out of his windscreen, through the massive propeller that was spinning so purposefully, it was his time to complete sixteen months of training and take to the skies in one of the most modern aircraft in service at the time. The ever reliable and dependable Hurricane was a true thoroughbred of the skies. As he opened up the throttle, Hurricane 2427 leapt forward with purpose and surged into the skies above Britain, and at its controls was a young man from a small market town in Cambridgeshire. Initially battling the overwhelming sense that the aircraft was flying him and not the other way around, Victor settled into the flight and began to marvel at Sydney Camm's creation. Powerful, responsive and purposeful, the Hurricane could turn like no other aircraft that he'd ever flown. Adding a few thousand feet to the recommended heights for a first flight, he started to perform some gentle aerobatics, feeling the weight of the G-force pushing him into his seat. After just over an hour of flight, he let down into the circuit, lowered his undercarriage and landed safely back at the airstrip at Hawarden. He was a Hurricane pilot.

Making the most of his time at No. 7 OTU, Victor would register twenty hours and forty minutes experience on type in just ten days. On

10 July 1940, the weight of the pressure experienced from Luftwaffe reached its tipping point and the Battle of Britain 'officially' began. Sergeant Victor Howard Ekins could not have timed his training any better. He was in the last batch of the pilots to fully experience and benefit from each stage of training before joining a squadron. As the battle began to rage, training time was slashed as the need for replacement pilots grew but Victor was as ready as he'd ever be. As the pilots gathered at Hawarden for the last time, they received their postings. Victor was to leave immediately for RAF Kenley to join the training flight of 111 Squadron.

3

RAF Kenley

Arriving at RAF Kenley on 15 July 1940, Victor found himself in a different world. This was an active front-line fighter base containing both 615 and 64 squadrons – both of which had already been in combat over France and during the evacuation at Dunkirk. Their pilots were experienced in battle and had proven to themselves and others that they had what it takes to handle the pressure and stress of combat. Victor was still an observer to this saga that was playing out in the skies above Britain. He had been sent to RAF Kenley to join the training section of 111 Squadron but wouldn't join the squadron for real until at RAF Croydon when their commander, Squadron Leader John 'Tommy' Thompson, deemed he was ready, or the need for replacement pilots got too great. While airborne with his squadron Victor would have the lives of his fellow pilots in his hands and they would have his life in theirs – it was essential that he could be relied upon.

So, for now, Victor waited on the sidelines as the heroes of the hour bravely rose to the challenge in the skies above Britain. He may have worn the same uniform as them, shared a base with them, even sat close to them in the mess hearing tales of aerial duels with the Luftwaffe, but as yet, he was not one of them. On 18 July 1940 he was able to get airborne in a Miles Magister for some local flying to familiarise himself with Kenley, before taking to the skies in a Hurricane once again on 22 July to practise formation flying. He focused fully on the task at hand knowing that in the very near future the greatest test of his life lay waiting for him.

The early phase of the Battle of Britain saw the Luftwaffe focus its attention on shipping convoys in the English Channel and on Channel ports but the word on everybody's lips throughout Britain was 'invasion'. They had seen the Nazi successes in Europe and knew it was only a matter of time before they would feel the might of the German forces. On 16 July, Hitler issued Directive No. 16, calling for preparations to be made for Operation Sea Lion – the planned invasion of Britain. In it he demanded that 'The British

Sergeant Victor Ekins, July 1940.

Air Force must be eliminated to such an extent that it will be incapable of putting up any sustained opposition to the invading troops.' Once air superiority had been gained the Luftwaffe could then cover the invading forces as they landed on various locations along the south coast from Kent to East Sussex. Landing barges had been prepared and readied along the French coast as the world watched on.

Any doubts that Hitler may have had about the prospect of invading Britain were calmed by one of his most trusted allies, Hermann Goering, the Commander-in-Chief of the Luftwaffe. He had seen his relatively new fighting force achieve stunning success during the Spanish Civil War, the invasion of Poland, Norway, the Low Countries, Belgium and France. They had only ever known victory and were the most combat-experienced air force in the world – not to mention the most confident. They were also superior in numbers and Goering was in absolutely no doubt about the Luftwaffe's ability to completely wipe out the Royal Air Force, gain air superiority and then protect the invasion force. It would have to be a decisive victory, however, as the weather conditions and changing tides presented a limited window of opportunity. Hitler wanted to force Britain into a position where it had no choice but to seek peace terms, leaving him free to consolidate Nazi Europe before focusing his attention on Germany's 'natural enemy' – Russia.

Germany's success in conquering mainland Europe also led to many tactical advantages for the Luftwaffe. The Battle of France had proven that unescorted German bombers made relatively easy targets for the nimble Spitfires and Hurricanes of Fighter Command but now this same bomber force could be escorted all the way to London by the Messerschmitt Bf 109 fighters of the Luftwaffe. Taking off from airfields along the French coast, the Bf 109, which was equal to its British counterparts, now had the range needed and enjoyed the tactical advantage of height and positioning before entering battle. Despite limitations in the length of time that they could stay and fight, the Bf 109 would either protect the German bombers as they destroyed RAF aircraft on the ground, or engage in combat with RAF squadrons above Britain and shoot them out of the skies. The fate of the free world hung on the outcome of the first battle in history to be waged solely in the air. Just 2,938 young airman from the Royal Air Force, with an average age of only 20 years old, stood between German success and the prospect of a Nazi 'Reich that would last for a thousand years'. Sergeant Victor Howard Ekins was one of them.

To counter this immense threat, Britain had developed the most modern and advanced defensive system anywhere in the world. Conceived by Air Chief Marshal Hugh Dowding, the AOC of Fighter Command, it proved to be absolutely vital to the successful defence of Britain in 1940. The 'Dowding System' consisted of an integrated air defence system that combined Radio Direction Finding (later known as RADAR) with the Observer Corps to build up a strategic picture of the situation in the air. Together they would form an early warning system as information about height, range and numbers would be passed down the line of communication to Fighter Command HQ at Bentley Priory and then shared among sector airfields, of which RAF Kenley was one. This information was then used to exercise operational control over the squadrons of Fighter Command by its controllers. The whole idea was to be able to get aircraft into the sky at the right place and time to meet the enemy attack, and all of this gathered intelligence and information was plotted on a huge map in the operations room. Once a decision was made, the controller would call the relevant squadron and give the order to 'scramble'. After they were airborne, the squadron would remain in contact with ground control, a resource that the Luftwaffe did not have, and would only cut contact once the enemy were sighted and the call sign 'Tally Ho' given. The German High Command never truly grasped the true value of this system and therefore never concentrated any real efforts to destroy it. The Radio Direction Finding (RDF) masts were a clear and obvious target but only the site at RAF Ventnor ever received any significant damage.

At the heart of Fighter Command's defensive system was the Women's Auxiliary Air Force. The WAAF's calm and efficient manner would come to define the understated strength that could be found on RAF bases across Britain. They covered a variety of different roles but those chosen for the rather vague job title of 'Clerk – Special Duties' would find themselves at the very forefront of 'the Dowding System'. These were the young women who were chosen to work within the operations room, and were, in fact, the only other people allowed into this most important space other than the controllers themselves. The WAAFs at RAF Kenley worked tirelessly, in a relentless shift pattern, and bore witness to the epic battle that raged overhead.

One specific role of a 'Clerk – Special Duties' was that of the 'Plotter'. They were stationed around a huge table in the middle of the operations room with a map of southern England upon it. Armed with a croupier-style plotting rod, they would transfer all of the relevant information onto small wooden counters and after placing

'Plotters' from the Women's Auxiliary Air Force at work in the operations room.

them onto the map and sliding them into position, were able to create an up-to-date picture of the situation in the air. They could see exactly which squadrons were airborne at any given time and, more importantly, the size and direction of the incoming threat. One such member of the WAAF who worked as a plotter within the ops room was a young lady called Margaret Kimber. Known to all who knew her as 'Kim', she was just 20 years old and had been posted to Kenley on 11 May 1940. She had a strong and adventurous personality and had spent the previous two years prior to the outbreak of war at a finishing school in Switzerland. Her special skills as noted by the RAF on enlistment were that she was proficient at first aid, spoke fluent French and drove a car. It was during this period of time when Victor was readying himself for the herculean task ahead that he first met his beloved 'Kim'.

Margaret 'Kim' Kimber, worked as a clerk 'Special Duties' with the Women's Auxiliary Air Force.

Victor once again sat in the cockpit of his Hurricane at the end of the concrete runway at RAF Kenley and awaited clearance to take off from the controller. Feeling that familiar vibration under his seat and seeing those purposeful wings either side complete with the unforgettable sight of the RAF roundels, he was about to take the last flight of his training. Alongside him were the other Hurricanes of 111 Training Squadron, arriving at their designated positions and readying themselves to get airborne for more formation flying. Looking left and right, he could not deny the sense of pride as the squadron's Rolls-Royce Merlin engines roared, impatient to get airborne and enter the world for which they were designed. At the controls of these aircraft were young men who, over the last thirteen days, had become Victor's friends. They included Flying Officer Hardman and Sergeant Wallace, who would also be making the move to Croydon, eager to prove themselves worthy and capable of doing their duty during this huge struggle.

Stories had filtered through over the past weeks of huge formations of enemy aircraft penetrating Britain's airspace and ruthlessly bombing airbases, factories and buildings. Of innocent lives being lost and epic dogfights as the squadrons of Fighter Command repelled attack after attack. They had heard the rumours of German invasion forces massing in France and reports of young men going down in flames, trapped in their burning aircraft desperately trying to stave off this threat. Despite this harrowing picture, Victor's biggest fear was quite simply the thought of letting his squadron down but he had resolved to do absolutely everything in his power not to let this happen. There was a steely determination inside him and an intense feeling of defiance.

It was now 31 July 1940 and during his time at Kenley, Victor had managed to add another eleven hours and thirty-five minutes of flight in the Hawker Hurricane, taking his total on type to thirty-two hours and fifteen minutes. He had practised formation flying, air-to-air combat and had had the opportunity to fire his guns for real at the Leysdown firing ranges. As this determined group of pilots purposely opened the throttles of their aircraft and took to the skies once again above Kenley, Victor reflected on the prospect of joining his squadron for real at RAF Croydon. No. 111 Squadron, known as 'Treble One', had been at the heart of the fighting since the very start of the conflict and were proving themselves to be a courageous group of warriors. Their squadron leader, John Thompson, was one of the earliest advocates of using high-risk head-on attacks to disperse these huge enemy formations, as a small number of Hurricanes would surge into the midst of hundreds of enemy aircraft, machine guns blazing. It was to this band of brothers that Victor would have to prove himself capable and able to do his duty – and he wouldn't have long to wait to find out if he was up to the task.

4

Treble One

On 1 August 1940, the Operational Record Book (ORB) of 111 Squadron simply notes 'Wallace and Ekins returned to Squadron from attachment at Kenley.' Victor had joined his squadron and moved the few miles to RAF Croydon. Croydon Airport had a long history of civil aviation dating back to 1920 and had become Britain's first major international airport but was closed at the outbreak of war and converted into one of the fighter stations given the task of protecting London from German bombing. Things seemed quiet on his arrival and after an initial enquiry Victor was informed that 'Treble One' were at their forward base at RAF Hawkinge. This was the closest base to occupied France and a variety of squadrons would fly down at first light and use Hawkinge to patrol the south coast and, in theory, offer a quick interception should any enemy raids appear. 'Treble One' would then fly back to Croydon as light faded, often in preparation for a few well-earned pints at their local pub, The Propeller, which was situated just outside the base.

As the Hurricanes came in to land one by one, Victor could clearly see the squadron codes JU painted on the sides. The canvas patches that covered the gunports, designed to stop the Browning machine guns from freezing, were still intact, meaning that the squadron had not engaged the enemy that day. As the returning aircraft came to a stop and the ever loyal and committed ground crews got to work, Victor began to meet the personalities with whom he would take to the skies over the coming weeks – and what a distinctive bunch

Hurricanes from 111 Squadron being refuelled.

they were. Many of these men were RAF regulars and had joined the squadron pre-war. Full of experience, they had proven themselves to be a courageous and determined group of airmen who were making a very real difference in the struggle that was taking place in the skies above Britain.

Victor was introduced to the commander of 'Treble One', Squadron Leader John 'Tommy' Thompson. He had joined the RAF in 1934 and took command of 111 Squadron in January 1940, immediately stamping his own philosophy and personality onto his new squadron. A man of considerable height and physique, Thompson was a keen sportsman who boxed and played rugby to a very high standard – he oozed fighting spirit. His size and manner could initially come across as quite intimidating but behind the impressive figure was a warm smile and charming personality. He was loved by his pilots. His directness, aggression, sense of duty and sheer levels of courage had inspired the squadron into becoming a unique and spirited fighting force. Throughout the Battle of France and the early exchanges in the Battle of Britain he had become one of the early pioneers of the head-on attack, as small numbers of Hurricanes would fly directly towards enemy formations, sometimes hundreds strong. This would have the result of spreading the formation far and wide, disrupting its ability to bomb its target successfully and, once separated, present an easier opportunity to attack. The German formations would lose the protection of 'the pack' and would be left with the unenviable task of either carrying on with their bombing run in smaller and ragged formations or ditching their bomb load and fighting their way back to their bases on the French coast. It was a highly successful tactic but it wasn't for the faint hearted.

Flying against daunting odds, into the withering crossfire of the German bombers, with the high chance of a head-on collision, presented a terrifying prospect. While other squadrons were still using the pre-set and completely out of date RAF tactics for attack or had used head-on attacks in isolated situations, 111 Squadron, with Squadron Leader Thompson at the helm, would go on to make it their standard. Where the situation in the air allowed, regardless of numbers, they would surge into the midst of these huge formations at terrifying closing speeds, guns blazing. The margin for error was minute but that didn't deter 'Treble One' from adopting this extremely high-risk, yet high-reward tactic and John Thompson led from the front. They had a job to do and that was to stop the Luftwaffe at *any* cost.

'Treble One' also had two extremely experienced flight commanders that they could count on. Flight Lieutenant Stanley Conners had joined the squadron on 27 June 1938 and commanded 'B' Flight, with Flight Lieutenant Robin Powell, who had initially served with 111 Squadron in 1936, commanding 'A' Flight. One man who had made a real name for himself during the previous epic few months was Flying Officer Henry Michael Ferriss. Known as 'Michael' to the squadron, he had

enjoyed huge success and already had eight confirmed aerial victories to his name, as well as three shared, two probable victories and two aircraft damaged. He had built a reputation as a calm individual who was just as capable of getting himself out of trouble as he was getting into it.

Two personalities that really struck Victor were the unique Fisher brothers. Educated at Eton and living a life full of adventure before war had broken out, Anthony and Basil had a real passion for flight that had seen them explore Europe in their own private aircraft. Anthony was the eldest brother and was a modest and rather shy individual whose personality would truly shine when he graced the dance floor. His younger brother, Basil, on the other

Flight Lieutenant Michael Ferriss. Photo credit Andy Saunders.

hand, was a real character. He had been one of Eton's real extroverts, was immensely popular and inspired respect and warmth from those he met. The two were inseparable.

As the introductions continued, Victor was informed that he would be joining 'A' Flight under the command of Flight Lieutenant Robin Powell. He would be airborne with both Fisher brothers, Michael Ferriss, a young Canadian named Robert Wilson and sergeants, Robert Sim, John Craig and William Dymond. All these pilots had been flying operationally with the squadron since before the Battle of Britain had begun. They were full of combat experience and had learned many important lessons that could be passed onto Victor.

Pilot officers, Basil and Anthony Fisher. Photo credit Andy Saunders.

He was in extremely good company. As the remainder of 'Treble One's' pilots arrived, the gathering moved to The Propeller pub, an establishment that Victor would get to know well over the coming months, and he was confronted with yet more faces. Young men in their early twenties, with pints of beer in hand 'shooting the line' about recent duels with the Luftwaffe. The smoke-filled pub, with its distinctive wood-panelled saloon bar, was full of personnel, including the WAAFs from RAF Kenley, who seemed to draw the attention of almost all the pilots.

That first day, 1 August 1940, had been like a whirlwind for Victor. A blur of faces and personalities, tactics and advice that he would need to digest very quickly if he was to survive the perils of aerial combat. He was grateful to retire to his room that evening and consider all

that he had learned about his new squadron. 'Treble One' had seemed an incredibly tight unit on the ground, which had clearly been gained through the unifying bond of combat. They were a brotherhood and Victor was about to enter their world fully and without limitation. He had signed up to serve with the Royal Air Force during Britain's darkest hour and the day of reckoning had finally come.

Victor, the inexperienced sergeant pilot, joins 111 Squadron.

At 1025 hours the following morning Sergeant Victor Ekins, along with Flying Officer Michael Ferriss, were airborne before the rest of the squadron. The flight gave Victor the chance to acclimatise himself with the surroundings of a new airbase and the opportunity to familiarise himself with his new aircraft, Hurricane 2888. Each machine had its own unique feel and, once accustomed to their new steed, pilots were loath to fly anything else. The flight, which lasted less than an hour, also gave Flying Officer Ferriss the chance to assess Victor's airmanship in preparation for him flying operationally with the squadron. Michael Ferriss came across as a very together and calm individual with a natural RT voice that put those who flew alongside him at ease. The pair landed and 'A' Flight was put at readiness, with Victor included on the flying roster along with Flying Officer Ferriss, Pilot Officer Anthony Fisher and sergeants, Sim, Dymond and Craig.

Shortly after midday, they were ordered to get airborne and move to their forward base at RAF Hawkinge. The Luftwaffe were still employing tactics of attacking shipping in the English Channel and this forward base offered the best opportunity for an interception. Victor was flying operationally with his squadron for the first time, grateful to be getting down to business. After patrolling RAF Hawkinge until their fuel levels were running low, the flight entered the circuit and landed without any enemy aircraft being sighted. They were scrambled twice more during the remainder of the afternoon but again, no interceptions were made and were eventually ordered back to RAF Croydon at 1810 hours. The day had proven to be highly successful for Victor as he was able to ease his way into operational squadron life but, deep down he was itching to prove himself against the enemy. He had been airborne five times over the course of the day, becoming more familiar with his new squadron with each flight.

On 3 August the squadron were ordered down to Hawkinge once again. Being airborne with the same pilots was reassuring as Victor began to recognise the individual traits of these experienced airmen. Some would sit low in their seats, hunched forward ready for combat.

Others would fly with their goggles on their forehead, sitting high in the cockpit for an improved field of vision and a greater chance of sighting their quarry. It was a thrill to be flying in formation with the other Hurricanes of the squadron, as each aircraft bobbed and jumped keeping station on one another's wing tip. There was a real sense of collective purpose as the squadron thundered south in search of the enemy but they endured another frustrating day waiting at dispersal for a call to scramble that did not come.

After completing five night landings on 4 August, a task that each pilot had to achieve, the squadron spent the next five days following a similar routine of flying down to Hawkinge and enduring frustrating calls to 'scramble' as the pilots of 'Treble One' would rise determinedly to their feet and sprint to their waiting aircraft only to be disappointed. Once airborne, despite much searching of the skies, the enemy could not be sighted. Victor had now undertaken twenty-four operational flights in his first eight days with the squadron but had yet to experience the adrenaline-fuelled tension of combat. During this period, Flight Lieutenant Powell had been posted away from the squadron to 7 OTU at Hawarden but this didn't stop Victor from beginning to feel like part of the team, and an extremely special team at that. Flying Officer Ferriss seamlessly stepped into the role of leading 'A' Flight as their bond tightened and relationships with the other pilots of 111 Squadron grew by the day, assisted in large part by evenings at The Propeller.

On Sunday, 11 August 1940 Victor was rostered off flying duties for a short period, giving him the chance to reflect on what had been an intense few months. As he watched the twelve Hurricanes take off and fly down to Hawkinge in squadron strength once again he was overcome by a sense of pride. It was an unforgettable sight as 111 Squadron, his squadron, were playing their part in this most important of quests – to preserve the freedom that the western world had come to enjoy. To stand up to the tyranny of a regime who were rampaging their way across Europe, imposing their will and philosophies on all who stood before them. The defiant streak within Victor flared up. He had an inner resolve to stand up to this threat and to play his part whatever the cost may be. It was, after all, his duty. For now though, he had been given a few days' break from operational flying and the chance to reconnect with loved ones and taste the almost foreign world of civilian life once again.

It cannot be underestimated how much luck and timing play their part during war. How seemingly insignificant decisions can have a massive impact on the future. Victor's short break away from RAF Croydon coincided exactly with a very definite change in tactic from the Luftwaffe. They had been testing the strength of the RAF by focusing on Channel ports and shipping over the preceding weeks, trying to entice British aircraft into the skies, but a more concerted effort would be needed if they were to successfully gain air superiority as a precursor to invasion. People on the south coast had become accustomed to the sights and sounds of aerial combat over the Channel and had been fascinated observers as the battle had raged but 11 August 1940 brought something new. A large build-up of German aircraft had been detected and plotted in the ops rooms across 11 Group, the largest so far, but controllers and plotters watched in horror as these huge formations began moving inland. Both Dover and Portland were bombed heavily as huge dogfights erupted across the south coast of Britain with every squadron in both 10 and 11 groups put on readiness. The pace of the attack persisted throughout the morning as pilots began to feel the strain of repeated calls to 'scramble', followed by intense combat in the air.

In the afternoon another large formation of enemy aircraft was picked up by RDF, this time heading towards the Thames Estuary to attack a shipping convoy that had just left the docks. No. 111 Squadron were scrambled from RAF Hawkinge and directed by ground control to intercept the enemy formation. Almost immediately, Flying Officer Hardman lost the function of his aircraft, leaving him no choice but to return to base and one of the Fisher brothers became detached and separated from the squadron. The remaining ten Hurricanes carried on their pursuit. As Squadron Leader Thompson followed the directions of the controller, a large formation of aircraft appeared ahead of them over Margate, as 'Treble One' readied themselves for the interception. Pilot Officer Jack Copeman was almost immediately set upon by a Bf 109 and was seen to spin slowly out of control before crashing into the sea. Flight Lieutenant Conners engaged a Bf 109 and was able to deliver a telling attack, seeing the aircraft also crash into the sea before having to break away from making further attacks on a second Bf 109 as his windscreen became covered in oil. He had no choice but to land at RAF Manston to have it cleaned. No. 111 Squadron were in the thick of it once again.

The remainder of the squadron had maintained a height of 15,000ft and were able to intercept a large formation of Dornier Do 215s, who put up a fierce resistance. Despite withering return fire, the Hurricanes pressed home their attack, trying to disrupt the formation but Pilot Officer John McKenzie's aircraft was hit by an escorting Bf 109 and the 20-year-old was tragically killed. Flying Officer Ferriss brought 'A' Flight into position for a head-on attack as the remaining aircraft of 111 Squadron launched themselves at the enemy, each pilot firing about 800 rounds of ammunition. Pilot Officer Robert Wilson and Sergeant Robert Sim were last seen pouring fire into the formation but they were both tragically killed in action, and presumed to have been shot down into the sea. They were 20 and 23 years old respectively. It had proved to be an immensely costly engagement for the young men of 111 Squadron as four of their pilots had been killed in a matter of minutes. The remains of the squadron reformed at RAF Hawkinge before making their way back to Croydon as light faded. Squadron Leader Thompson would go on to write the following note to the family of Robert Wilson:

'I have been waiting until now hoping to hear some news of Bobby but have heard nothing. I am terribly sorry to have to tell you that there is not much hope of seeing him again.'

Sunday, 11 August 1940 proved to be the costliest day of the entire battle in terms of loss of life for the pilots of Fighter Command, with twenty-five airmen being killed in action. No. 111 Squadron had been rocked by the death of four of its pilots with whom Victor had been airborne only the day before. The Luftwaffe began to ramp up the pressure it was exerting on Britain, making a determined effort to knock out the Royal Air Force, and it was only the beginning.

The following day, 'Treble One' was up at dawn and flew down to Hawkinge through an early morning mist. There they waited, weary but ready for what the day may have in store as the sun began to shine, revealing yet another beautiful summer's day. The morning of 12 August saw the next phase of the Luftwaffe's plan really kick into gear. Their aim was simple – knockout British RDF stations and masts, removing the early warning of attack, and begin to systematically destroy RAF bases across the south of England. Throughout the morning, pinpoint low-level attacks came in one after another at Dover, Rye, Pevensey and Ventnor stations, leading the Luftwaffe commanders to believe that they had left the RAF 'without their eyes'. The reality of the matter, however, was that, despite each station experiencing significant damage and suffering loss of life, they were back online in a matter of hours, with the exception of Ventnor.

The morning attack was concluded with the bombing of both Portsmouth and Southampton as the Supermarine works was targeted in an attempt to disrupt the production of the Spitfire. No. 111 Squadron were airborne multiple times throughout the morning without meeting the enemy and were ordered back to Croydon early in the afternoon. Shortly afterwards the bases at Manston, Lympne and Hawkinge were badly hit, with Hawkinge sustaining severe damage to hangars and buildings that put it out of action for a number of days. 'Treble One' flew multiple sorties from RAF Croydon throughout the afternoon, with many pilots being airborne for almost seven hours since their dawn take-off but, despite enemy aircraft being sighted, no interceptions were made.

The morning of 13 August dawned cloudy and overcast. The Commander of the Luftwaffe, Hermann Goering, had given it the code name Eagle Day or 'Adler Tag' and identified it as the start of the first major assault on Britain. He was determined to press home the attack and had planned out a day's offensive that began at dawn and would continue into the night. The German formations that would fly over Britain would be the largest seen up until this point, as they sought to destroy Fighter Command once and for all. Despite being exhausted and having lost experienced pilots over the preceding weeks, the squadrons of the RAF were still very much in the fight. Luftwaffe intelligence had massively exaggerated the losses suffered by Fighter Command since the battle had begun, also believing its infrastructure to be on its knees and RDF destroyed. Poor weather over the French coast, combined with slow communication between German commanders, led to mass confusion throughout the German forces. An order to cancel the attack hadn't been received, leading to the day's offensive getting off to a very disjointed start. Nevertheless, as early as 0640 hours the battle erupted in the skies above Britain.

Kim was on duty at RAF Kenley that morning and could see these huge raids as they developed on the map in the operations room. She and Victor had been growing closer over the previous weeks and their relationship had developed during those memorable nights at The Propeller. She was in the unenviable position of seeing exactly where 111 Squadron were at any given time and, more importantly, the scale of the enemy formations that they were being asked to intercept. This sense of jeopardy and then sheer relief when they were able to meet once again was adding a depth to their relationship that would be almost impossible to understand unless you had shared their experience. As she plotted raid after raid on the morning of 13 August, the controller at RAF Kenley 'scrambled' 111 Squadron.

In full squadron strength, they were ordered to intercept an enemy raid that was attacking RAF Eastchurch. Squadron Leader Thompson led 'Treble One' as they tore into a formation of Dorniers that had been sighted flying down the Thames Estuary, using the tried and tested head-on attack to scatter the enemy formation across the sky. Flying Officer Ferriss, who was once again leading 'A' Flight, managed to send one of the enemy aircraft down in flames as the squadron were able to bring home a series of successful attacks. This was followed by further victories for Squadron Leader Thompson, Pilot Officer McIntyre, Pilot Officer Walker and a shared claim for sergeants, Dymond and Craig. No. 111 Squadron had destroyed five enemy aircraft with only slight damage to their own and it proved to be a sign of things to come for the Luftwaffe throughout the remainder of 'Eagle Day'. As the day's epic events drew to a close, it was clear that it had been a total disaster for the Luftwaffe as Fighter Command had successfully kept German forces at bay with relatively few losses. Goering had started the day believing that the Royal Air Force was close to collapse but had been proved very wrong indeed. A more decisive effort would be needed if he was to prevail.

5

Into the Fray

The following day saw a slower pace as the Luftwaffe regrouped. 'Treble One' was scrambled multiple times without engaging the enemy and received the welcome news that Flying Officer Michael Ferriss had been promoted to flight lieutenant, officially taking over 'A' Flight. Victor was due to return to RAF Croydon on 15 August and couldn't wait to reconnect with his squadron after his brief time away. Civilian life didn't seem the same now he'd been introduced to the camaraderie and fellowship of a front-line fighter squadron. He had last flown with the squadron on 10 August but a mere four days seemed to have changed everything. He had left with a sense of frustration, enduring multiple scrambles and patrols without incident, but would return that Thursday afternoon under the immediate shadow of war to the news that many of his friends had been lost. Things had become personal for Victor.

The Luftwaffe were now determined to press home the attack that had promised so much but failed so miserably on Eagle Day. On 15 August they had regrouped and were prepared for a full-scale assault in yet larger numbers that would take place the length of Britain. German bombers based in Norway were now joining the battle by attacking RAF bases in the north of England. At 1100 hours the onslaught across the Channel began and huge dogfights developed across the south of the country. The air was full of twisting and turning aircraft duelling and fighting until the last as a Herculean effort was being made by airmen from both halves of the conflict. Observers looked on in amazement as burning aircraft descended from above and parachutes seemed to litter the sky. Young men were throwing themselves into battle, often suffering severe injuries and burns as the demands of the Battle of Britain hit fever pitch.

Victor had arrived back at RAF Croydon that afternoon just in time to see 111 Squadron scramble to intercept nearly 300 German aircraft that had been plotted by ops rooms across 11 Group. As they gained height, the pilots of 'Treble One' couldn't help but identify this vast aerial armada, which seemed almost impenetrable. Full of courage and determination, they did what they could against daunting odds. Everything happened so fast as the sky turned into a mix of whirling aircraft. Each time it seemed like they had the enemy in their sights, they'd have to almost immediately break off the attack as their own aircraft came under fire. The intensity, the heat of the battle, the nerves and the constant swivelling of their necks looking out for enemy aircraft added to the tension. Calls over the RT from squadron members warning one another, sometimes forlornly, of incoming attacks, as images of the Black Crosses of German aircraft flashed past the windscreen and were ingrained into the mind. In among this chaos the squadron managed to shoot down four enemy machines for no loss before the battle began to dissipate. Each pilot who knew aerial combat also knew the eerie feeling of one minute experiencing a sky full of aircraft, the next being completely alone and isolated as the battle seemed to disappear. This was one of the quirks of waging war in three dimensions.

The exhausted pilots from 'Treble One' landed one by one and were pleased to hear that, despite three Hurricanes being damaged, no one had been killed. They drew breath as the aircraft were rearmed and refuelled, smoking cigarettes and excitedly reporting their victories to the squadron's intelligence officer. Victor was desperate to get involved but almost as soon as the squadron were refuelled, the phone rang and the shouted command to 'scramble' was heard. The pilots of 'Treble One' dropped everything and rushed to their aircraft, forming up and surging once again into the dangerous skies above. This time, they were vectored south by controllers and directed towards another enemy raid that had crossed the coast and was moving purposefully inland. Over Selsey Bill the two formations clashed and 111 Squadron did the only thing they knew under these circumstances – pressed home the head-on attack. Into the German aircraft they went, machine guns blazing as the Junkers Ju 88s and Bf 110s of the invading force were spread out across the sky. Almost instinctively both Anthony and Basil Fisher formed up together and started to attack a Ju 88, which put up a strong resistance. The brothers took it in turn to fire at the aircraft, which was seen to spiral out of control and crash near Thorney Island. Within seconds of their shared victory, success was replaced by tragedy as Basil Fisher's Hurricane was hit by enemy fire, with his brother looking on helplessly. Anthony could clearly see his brother's aircraft going up in flames as he strived to give whatever protection he could amidst the chaos of battle. Basil fought hard to free himself from the stricken aircraft as Anthony's Hurricane flew alongside and he could be seen to slowly open the canopy. Eventually he hauled himself clear and descended into the open air, pulling the ripcord of his parachute. Despite initially deploying, Anthony watched in horror as Basil's parachute began to burn, having caught alight as he battled to free himself from the blaze. Slowly, the fire travelled to the harness straps and Anthony Fisher witnessed the horrific sight of his younger brother free-falling to his death.

The squadron landed at RAF Croydon yet again exhausted from combat, and heard the tragic news of Basil Fisher's death. This really was the day of days for 111 Squadron. As the ground crews hurriedly rearmed and refuelled the aircraft, pilots from 'Treble One' grabbed a brew where they could and tried to gather their thoughts. News had been filtering through about the day's attacks by the Luftwaffe as every squadron in the south-east of England had gone into combat. Within minutes of landing and rearming, the phone rang once more and there was yet another call to 'Scramble!'. It was now 1850 hours. The battle-weary pilots summoned what energy they had left, hauled themselves to their feet and dashed towards their aircraft. Incredibly, Anthony Fisher was one of them, as once again 'Treble One' took to the skies.

Victor had been talking to Sergeant Cyril 'Ted' Hampshire, who had arrived from 85 Squadron as a much-needed replacement pilot and had just reported for duty. The pair ran outside to see the Hurricanes scramble, clawing for height and being almost immediately confronted by the sight of twenty-two Bf 110s of the crack *Erprobungsgruppe* 210 unit commanded by Hauptmann W. Rubensdörffer. The sight of the 'Treble One' Hurricanes had taken Rubensdörffer completely by surprise as his experienced squadron had just started their bombing run with RAF Croydon itself being the target. Explosions rang out around the aerodrome and surrounding suburbs as the chaos of battle once again descended on 111 Squadron. Victor and Ted threw themselves to the floor as the ground shook under the deafening power of the attack. Buildings exploded and windows smashed, as shrapnel and debris filled the air around them. All of a sudden there was another deafening boom as one of the Bf 110s managed to score a direct hit on the airfield's armoury, the blast being heard as far away as the Houses of Parliament. A hangar on the far side of the airfield exploded and began burning with such ferocity that it took a number of days to get it under control. The feeling of vulnerability combined with sheer anger filled Victor's body. If war had at all seemed distant with the frustrations of unsuccessful scrambles and patrols, then here, on 15 August 1940, it became a reality.

It's a miracle that 111 Squadron had managed to get airborne at all under such circumstances but as they gained height, their minds became clear and focused. This was personal. The bombs that were raining down on RAF Croydon and the surrounding areas were killing their own and they were damned if they were going to let it continue. As Squadron Leader Thompson brought his men into position, they were confronted by the welcome sight of Hurricanes from 32 Squadron, which had been scrambled from RAF Biggin Hill. With bodies braced and teeth gritted, they threw themselves at the invaders. The Bf 110s did the only thing they could to defend against attack from fighters, which was to form up into a defensive circle, but even that wasn't enough to stop the Hurricanes of Fighter Command. Four enemy machines were destroyed by 'Treble One', with Squadron Leader Thompson, Flight Lieutenant Connors and Sergeant Wallace among the pilots to make claims. The Bf 110s were hounded all the way to the south coast by 32 and 111 squadrons, with Hauptmann W. Rubensdörffer himself shot down and killed. It had been a costly day for the Luftwaffe, which would go on to be known in Germany as 'Black Thursday' – the day where they had experienced their most severe losses.

Returning one by one to RAF Croydon after this intense combat, the pilots of 111 Squadron found it ablaze and in a terrible state. After landing with some difficulty, they took stock. Within the space of a mere hour, the life of Pilot Officer Anthony Fisher had changed forever. Inconsolable after the horrific circumstances surrounding his brother's death, he arrived back at Croydon to find the sleeping quarters that he had so recently shared with Basil completely destroyed. All of their belongings were gone, including both of their flying logbooks. If these events hadn't been tragic enough, of the six people who were killed on the aerodrome, five belonged to 111 Squadron, including members of both of the brothers' ground crews. It was simply too much for a young man to bear. Pilot Officer Anthony Fisher was immediately placed on leave suffering from extreme trauma and a nervous breakdown – he would never fly operationally again. He was to bury his brother five days later, on 20 August 1940, the same day Prime Minister Winston Churchill first publicly uttered the immortal words: 'Never in the field of human conflict, was so much owed, by so many, to so few.' This was the brutal reality of the Battle of Britain.

The events of 15 August had left a huge mark on 111 Squadron. The stresses and strains of battle were becoming evident, along with the weight of loss to friends and colleagues alike. The only thing that the pilots of 'Treble One' could do was to put it out of their minds and carry on. Victor would emerge from the rubble to find all of his belongings gone, his car destroyed and his pilot's logbook missing. This would later be found in the debris, covered with scorch marks as it sat tantalisingly close to the fires that burnt around Croydon. The raid by Hauptmann Rubensdörffer was a very controversial attack that

 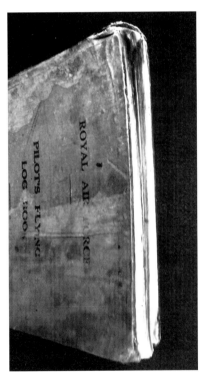

Above left: Victor's original pilot logbook that was lost during the bombing of RAF Croydon on 15 August 1940.

Above right: Now on display at the Kent Battle of Britain Museum, you can clearly see the scorch marks as it sat tantalisingly close to the flames.

would go on to have long-lasting consequences. It has been reported that he identified RAF Croydon by mistake due to weather conditions, his original target being RAF Kenley. Rubensdörffer had been a pre-war Lufthansa commercial airline pilot and had flown to Croydon Airport many times; whether he could have mistaken an airport that he'd visited so often will never be proven. What is known for a fact, however, is that the raid caused huge damage to the factories and suburbs surrounding RAF Croydon and killed sixty innocent people, injuring a further 180. It was the first time that Londoners had been affected by bombing, despite Hitler's express orders not to attack the capital.

The pace of those unforgettable summer days during 1940 was absolutely relentless. Victor would take to the skies once again on 16 August flying in Hurricane 3106 as the squadron made its way south to Hawkinge. Only ten aircraft were in a serviceable condition that day to make the flight and 'A' Flight could only muster four pilots instead of the usual six. They were the newly promoted Flight Lieutenant Ferriss and sergeants, Craig, Dymond and Ekins. After the previous day's events, the pilots were desperately in need of a rest and they lay basking in the sun near the dispersal hut at Hawkinge, taking whatever downtime they could. At around 1150 hours their brief moment of peace abruptly ended when the telephone rang and the pilots were ordered to scramble. Victor rose to his feet and dashed the 50 yards to his waiting aircraft in the quickest time that he could physically manage. Into the cockpit he went, clipping on his face mask, turning on the oxygen flow and giving the ground crew the thumbs up for 'chocks away'. The Rolls-Royce Merlin engine roared into life and, forming up with the other aircraft from 'A' Flight, he took to the skies in search of the enemy. Three large raids had been plotted by ops rooms that day but the largest by far was approaching the south coast near Dungeness.

As Squadron Leader Thompson led 'Treble One' onto the vector given to him by controllers, he could see another Hurricane squadron climbing steeply to port and also a distant squadron of what looked like Spitfires. They were all heading in the same direction, that being towards a swarm of Dornier Do 215s that had appeared on the horizon, escorted by a large number of Bf 109s, around 200 enemy aircraft in total. Flight Lieutenant Ferriss, speaking calmly over the RT, readied the remains of 'A' Flight for a head-on attack as the four Hurricanes braced themselves for combat.

Sergeant Victor Ekins.

The closing speed was incredible as Victor determinedly pressed the gun button and his eight Browning machine guns roared into life. In a matter of seconds, he was forced to break off his attack, doing everything in his power to avoid a head-on collision as a Dornier passed within what seemed like inches. This daring attack had broken up a large part of the enemy formation as the three squadrons from Fighter Command pounced but it had had huge consequences. On only his second day as a flight lieutenant, the stalwart of 'Treble One' and Victor's flight commander, Michael Ferriss, was killed. The fine margins of the head-on attack had finally caught up with him and he is believed to have collided with one of the Dorniers. It was yet another tremendous blow to 'Treble One' and 'A' Flight in particular as they had lost both Fisher brothers and now Ferriss in less than twenty-four hours.

As mass dogfights broke out over Dungeness, Sergeant Craig was able to claim a Dornier as destroyed, which was seen to crash at Tunbridge Wells. Sergeant Wallace found himself in a head-on battle with a Bf 109 as both pilots, fully committed, flew at each other at full speed with guns blazing. By sheer grit and a little luck, he was able to shoot it down and see it crash into the sea. Sergeant Carnall was not so lucky. He had been attacked and his Hurricane had almost instantly caught fire, leaving him no choice but to frantically try to escape the burning aircraft. He managed to bail out but had sustained horrific injuries and would go on to spend a year in hospital undergoing plastic surgery for his burns. He was treated by Archibald McIndoe and became a member of the legendary 'Guinea Pig Club'.

The pilots of 111 Squadron arrived back at RAF Croydon that afternoon and, yet again, had to count the cost of battle. The squadron were being decimated but the demands placed on Fighter Command during August 1940 meant that they had no choice but to carry on with the fight. The following day proved to be a perfect English summer's day as Victor and the rest of 'A' Flight, which now contained only sergeant pilots, flew down to Hawkinge for another day of tension and waiting but the call to scramble never came. That day, 17 August, proved to be one of the quietest days of the battle so far with no casualties recorded for Fighter Command. Sergeants, Albert Deacon and Frank 'Harry' Silk, arrived at RAF Croydon as much-needed replacement pilots and the squadron speculated why they had been given a day's reprieve by the Luftwaffe. The following day's events would prove that it was merely the calm before the storm.

6

The Hardest Day

As Kim cycled with her good friend and fellow WAAF, Eileen Whiteman, through the country lanes leading to RAF Kenley they were struck by the beauty of the day. Sunday, 18 August 1940 had brought a peaceful summer morning that, along with the previous day's lull in fighting, had given them a brief respite from the tension and pressure of five weeks of battle. Working in the sector operations room at RAF Kenley had placed them in one of the strategic epicentres of the conflict, with relentless shift rotation and the day-to-day demands of being directly involved in this huge struggle for freedom. Due to the nature of their work, the previous weeks had seen the WAAFs develop a very personal rapport with the pilots from squadrons based around London. They would plot on the huge map in the operations room the progress of the squadrons as they were regularly called into action against daunting odds and, as a result, a feeling of togetherness and affection grew under the dark clouds of war.

Their current shift rotation meant a slightly later start to their day, the opportunity to be outdoors and a chance to chat. Although it was easy to forget given the responsibility placed upon their shoulders, they were two young women in their early twenties with a lot to talk about. As the gentle summer's breeze swept into Kim's face, she began chatting about Victor and the feelings that were developing for this young man. Their friendship had blossomed over previous weeks, having enjoyed nights out at The Propeller pub and the Davis Cinema in Croydon. The Davis Cinema was fast becoming a favourite haunt for pilots and

WAAFs alike as a one shilling and sixpence ticket would buy entry to a double feature programme, tea in the restaurant and then access to the dance that would go on into the night. It was a blissful escape from the intensity of those summer days of 1940. Eileen Whiteman also had plenty to talk about as she had recently met a young man called 'Jim' who had been making quite a name for himself flying with 501 Squadron. As the pair chatted, lost in their own world while cycling through the country lanes with the sun in their faces, the sight of the main gates of RAF Kenley came into view ahead.

This beautiful summer's weather was a lot harder to enjoy for Victor and the pilots of Fighter Command as it meant favourable airborne conditions for an attack by the Luftwaffe and the promise of yet more fighting. 'Treble One' had been up since dawn and were waiting at dispersal for the first scramble of the day to come. The atmosphere was notably more subdued as each exhausted pilot processed and reacted to the events of the tumultuous last few days. There was, of course, the usual hustle and bustle of a front-line fighter base as ground crews readied the aircraft and the squadron prepared itself for battle but the banter between pilots had a hollow quality and the conversation was muted. So much had happened to 111 Squadron over the previous week, with constant changes to flying personnel, the nerve-wracking pressure of aerial combat and the tragic loss of life to friends and colleagues starting to take its toll. Victor was a man of great strength who never gave the impression of being worried but the baptism of fire that he'd experienced over the last few weeks was proving hard to process even for him. The squadron had received a telegram on the morning of 18 August from Air Chief Marshal Cyril Newell congratulating them on their successes and continued fighting spirit, but even this well-intended note of encouragement had missed the mark.

Despite these precious moments of solitude and reflection, Victor could sense that something was brewing and that soon the squadron would be airborne once again. The unforgettable and nerve-jangling sound of the telephone ringing had begun and Squadron Leader

Thompson was up on his feet, noticeably preoccupied with what had been reported to him. What a leader he was. From the moment Victor had joined the squadron a mere eighteen days ago, which actually felt like a lifetime, John Thompson had led from the front with complete disregard for his own safety. He was steadfastly focused on the fact that 'Treble One' had a job to do and that was to stop the Luftwaffe at all costs – it was as simple as that. As the phone rang yet again, Victor watched on as his squadron leader listened intently to what was being reported to him. He placed the phone down determinedly and turned to his squadron. A large raid had been plotted heading across the Channel and 111 Squadron had been brought to readiness and asked to stand by in their aircraft. Fighter Command were still unsure of the exact target of the latest raid but it was clear that very soon they would be called upon and imminently enough for them to have to sit in their cockpits and wait with engines running. In the absence of Michael Ferriss, Pilot Officer James Walker was to lead 'A' Flight with sergeants, Craig, Ekins, Dymond, Hampshire and Deacon, making up the rest of the formation. They had also been told the welcome news that an experienced pilot, Flight Lieutenant Giddings, was on his way to take over the section.

Victor got to his feet and walked the short distance to his waiting aircraft. He had been airborne in Hurricane 2888 twenty-six times since his arrival at the squadron and had built a real affinity with this most dependable of steeds. His ground crew were diligently working on 'their' aircraft and welcomed Victor's arrival with the usual rundown of the latest state of the Hurricane. What a team they all made. With his parachute already on, he climbed up onto the walkway of the wing and once again into the familiar surroundings of the cockpit, settling himself down as best he could. Pulling the Sutton harness straps over his shoulders and tightening them to the point of being just on the right side of uncomfortable, Victor pulled on his flying helmet, fixed the mask, checked the oxygen flow and turned on his RT. The familiar smells of the cockpit and the exactitude of the routine began to settle the nerves and almost instinctively his mind focused on the task in hand. The Rolls-Royce Merlin engine turned and spluttered before bursting into life and a quick thumbs up to his waiting ground crew signalled 'chocks away'. The aircraft trembled with impatience as the slipstream flattened the grass behind and Victor looked across to see the remainder of the squadron ready for action. These were unforgettable memories that would ingrain into his mind. The tension and anticipation of the moment was broken as Squadron Leader Thompson's voice crackled over the RT to report their readiness to Fighter Command and impatiently request permission to take off. There, on the runway at RAF Croydon, they waited, knowing that soon they would be asked to climb into hostile skies once again, and not knowing if they would be lucky enough to return.

On the airfields in northern France, pilots from the Luftwaffe had had an intense morning as they prepared for the day's attack on the airbases of Fighter Command. The Luftwaffe's plan to destroy the RAF on the ground and achieve a quick victory hadn't materialised, and frustration was growing throughout its commanders – time was of the essence. On the morning of 18 August they had briefed their pilots and crews of the need for a more concentrated attack that involved two airfields in particular – RAF Biggin Hill and RAF Kenley. The plan was to completely destroy both air bases with a complex and potentially destructive strategy and then, once successful, replicate the attack on the remaining bases of Fighter Command. After these initial raids of the day, attacks were planned on different targets throughout the rest of the afternoon and into the night. It was shaping up to be an important day for the Luftwaffe as they continued their efforts to clear the skies above Britain as a precursor to invasion. A measure of how memorable they thought the day was going to be can be seen in the decision to invite the 4th War Reporter Detachment and include eight reporters and photographers on the raids. War reporter, Georg Hinze, and photographer, Rolf von Pebal, stood by and watched as the detailed battle plan was revealed.

Initially, RAF Kenley was to be hit by an accurate dive-bombing attack from twelve Junkers Ju 88s, to be followed within minutes by a high-level bombing raid by twenty-seven Dornier Do 17s. To complete this pincer move and really bring home the attack, a further nine Do 17s would fly at no more than 50ft, remain undetected by RDF and approach Kenley from the south. Following the smoke from the damage of the previous raids, they would go on to destroy what was left of RAF Kenley. A larger raid of sixty Heinkel He 111s would focus on Biggin Hill, with all of the bombing forces except the low-flying Dorniers to fly behind a protective shield of free-hunting Bf 109s. Rolf von Pebal describes 'great tension' as pilots and crews boarded their aircraft in preparation for the momentous day ahead. Both he and George Hinze were to fly with 9th Staffel and the low-flying Dorniers.

Despite the perfect conditions over England, there had been heavy cloud cover over France, meaning the raid got off to a slow start with an initial hour's delay. Eventually all aircraft got airborne and began to form up but again flying conditions hampered the formations, drastically impacting the timings of this precision attack. The only aircraft to get airborne and begin their journey as expected were the nine low-flying Dornier 17s as they took station on one another's wing tips and thundered over the Channel at a daunting 15ft. They were now ominously in the lead and would prove to be the first bombers on the scene, instead of the last. Rolf von Pebal took what photos he could as the nine aircraft sighted Beachy Head and turned inland for the journey north to Kenley. The plan was quite simply to pick up the Brighton to London railway line, keep it on the left-hand side of the bombers and that would lead them all the way to Kenley. Rolf von Pebal would go on to write the following account:

> We are buzzing along at 300 kilometres per hour at an altitude of five metres over the English countryside. Every terrain elevation provides us with cover, every forest is used as concealment. We leap over trees; it is a continuous up and down movement. I see no flak emplacements. An express train passes under us and is gone, a pair riding

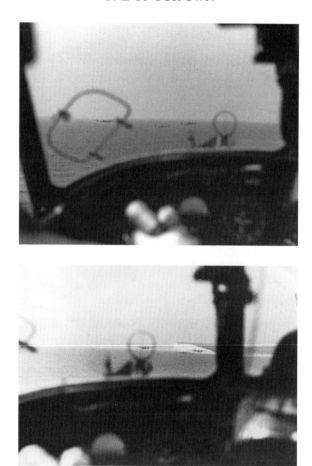

Above and opposite: The pictures taken by German war photographer, Rolf Von Pebal, on the journey to attack RAF Kenley, 18 August 1940. Photo credit Chris Goss.

bicycles takes cover in a ditch as if they were in basic training. Over parking areas, mansions, castles, factories and soot-darkened workers' houses – we race past. Those that see the Balkan Cross on our wings are gripped by panic.

Back at Fighter Command the large raid heading inland near Dover had been picked up by RDF and the Observer Corps, with squadrons from across 11 Group being scrambled to intercept. Both 32 and 610 squadrons from Biggin Hill and 64 and 615 squadrons from Kenley rose into these uncertain skies and were vectored to a higher altitude but this left the low-flying Dorniers unaccounted for and both bases open to attack. Reports were coming in from visual sightings of the aircraft but still a definite destination could not be confirmed as each airfield around London represented a possible target. Crucially, 111 Squadron remained in their aircraft at RAF Croydon. They were now the only possible option to defend against this low-level attack and time was most definitely of the essence. Eventually they were scrambled and the twelve Hurricanes rose purposefully into the skies, their pilots partly frustrated by the wait but also full of anticipation for what was to come. The aircraft bobbed and weaved as Squadron Leader Thompson began the climb to 20,000ft with orders to patrol base. Such was the confusion over the attack, they were then ordered down to 5,000ft and as further reports came in of the low-flying Dorniers, down further still to 3,000ft, with RAF Kenley being the destination.

As Kim and Eileen cycled through the main gates at Kenley and onto base their conversation was broken by a heavy rumbling sound that was getting louder and louder. They were, of course, used to the sound of aircraft above Kenley but this was different somehow and the two slowed down on their bikes to stare skywards. To their utter shock and amazement, nine enemy aircraft came into view, flying so low that they could make out the faces of the crew. There they stood, now rooted to the spot as the bombs began to rain down on Kenley. Explosions rang out across the aerodrome as a frantic call to 'Take cover!' snapped them back to reality and they scrambled into a nearby ditch. The raid had been so quick and unexpected that there was no thought of getting to a shelter; people on the ground at Kenley took whatever cover they could. As Kim peeked over the crest of the ditch, she watched in amazement as the Dorniers attacked her base, hotly pursued by a squadron of Hurricanes.

'Treble One' had been flying over RAF Kenley at 3,000ft when they spotted the enemy raid coming in. As Victor half-rolled his Hurricane and began to dive in for the attack he sighted the aircraft as they approached their target. Victor was a very fair man but on 18 August 1940, the Luftwaffe and, in particular, the pilots from 9 Staffel crossed a line. They were not only attacking an airbase of Fighter Command but they were also attacking Kim. His body braced and his jaw clenched at the very thought of it. This young lady who was beginning to mean so much to him, proving to be such amazing company with her strong and vibrant personality, was being bombed by the Luftwaffe. It had become very personal and a real hatred for his enemy stirred. Down the Hurricanes dived, throwing themselves into battle over Kenley.

Flight Lieutenant Conners, who was leading 'B' Flight, surged into the formation first, closely followed by Pilot Officer Simpson, and was sighted to be flying in the middle of the enemy bombers with Dorniers either side of him. The two Hurricanes ignored the return fire and focused all their attention on attacking the leader of the formation, who was destroyed. The anti-aircraft guns around the airbase opened up along with the machine gun defences as the skies criss-crossed with bullets flying in all directions. It was a confused scene of chaos as the bombs fell and buildings and hangars began to explode. Tragically, Flight Lieutenant Conners was trapped in this inferno and his Hurricane was hit. It's unclear in among the chaos whether it was by return fire from one of the raiding

A Spitfire sustains damage whilst in its dispersal pen at RAF Kenley from the low level attack on 18 August.

Dorniers or Kenley's own anti-aircraft fire but Conners was seen to pull away sharply before crashing, and sadly he was killed. He had been an absolute rock for 111 Squadron since Victor's arrival and they would never truly recover from his loss. Pilot Officer Simpson, who had only rejoined the squadron that morning, was also badly hit and was forced to crash land his Hurricane at the golf course of the Royal Automotive Club at Woodcote Park but thankfully emerged unscathed.

Despite the immediate response from 111 Squadron, the bombing had been extremely accurate by the Dorniers of 9th Staffel and the damage severe. Three hangars had been destroyed and had turned into a raging inferno along with the station headquarters and hospital. The operations room that Kim had got to know so well over the previous months had also been silenced and the damage caused to communication lines so extreme that it was never used operationally again. The Dorniers had also littered the airfield with delayed fuse bombs, which bounced over the grass before finding their resting place.

Sergeant Craig led Victor into the fray and claimed a further Dornier as 'probably' destroyed. Sergeants Dymond and Brown, led their sections down into the attack and after a fierce battle managed to account for a further two Dorniers as the German aircraft broke off the attack and made for home. They scattered in all directions and hugged the countryside to try and find whatever cover they could but it wasn't enough to dissuade the Hurricanes. Sergeant Newton found himself on the tail of one of the enemy machines and after a few short

Dornier Do 17 Z-2, coded F1+HT of 9/KG 76, crashed at 'Sunnycroft', Golf Road, Kenley, Surrey at 1320 hours on 18 August 1940.

bursts was about to deliver a telling blow, when his Hurricane was hit by return fire and burst into flames. The hood had been opened before the engagement, which had the effect of drawing the flames up and out of the aircraft, engulfing Newton who was still strapped in. As he grappled to free himself, the oxygen in his face mask caught fire, which melted and burnt onto his face. Adamant that he wouldn't lose his eyesight, he shut his eyes tightly but was suddenly gripped by an overwhelming sense of anger and rage at the thought of the Dornier getting away after causing so much damage to RAF Kenley. It seemed so unjust. Still within range of the enemy aircraft and with eyes closed, Sergeant Newton plunged his hands back into the flames, felt around for the control column, made a slight alteration to his course and then unleashed the eight Browning machine guns in the direction of his foe. Incredibly, this parting gesture of defiance found its mark but the inferno had by now burnt through his trousers, flying suit and gloves, and Sergeant Newton belatedly exited the Hurricane. The injuries that he sustained would keep the 19-year-old out of action for months.

As this first phase of the assault on Kenley came to an end and as those on the ground slowly began to resurface after the terrifying ordeal, bombs once again began to fall on the air base. The time was 1327 hours and the epic events of the first raid had taken place in the space of a mere five minutes but now it was the turn of the high-flying Dorniers to find their mark. People dashed for cover once more as RAF Kenley was engulfed in flames, smoke and debris. The skies above England were a mass of twisting aircraft as huge dogfights broke out across a vast front. RAF Biggin Hill was next on the hit list to suffer at the hands of the Luftwaffe but the RAF pilots remained defiant and threw themselves into battle. Sergeant Deacon had attacked a low-flying Dornier, expended all of his ammunition and had no choice but to land at RAF Croydon to rearm. In the confusion of events, the aerodrome's defences opened up and attacked Deacon with a viciously accurate burst, seriously wounding

RAF Kenley under attack during 'The Hardest Day', 18 August 1940. The church that is visible in the foreground is St Andrew's in Coulsdon. (Historic Military Press)

him in the legs. He had no choice but to bail out at a mere 200ft and was immediately rushed to hospital. Once again, 'Treble One' were at the forefront of the battle and its exhausted pilots were paying the price. To emphasise this, Flight Lieutenant Giddings, who had been posted to the squadron, was trying to join up with 'Treble One' but became embroiled in the melee of aircraft, with the ORB reporting that he 'arrived having shot down a Ju 88 on the way'.

As the dust settled over RAF Kenley after this most intense second raid, Kim and Eileen dragged themselves from the makeshift cover of the ditch and were shocked by the scene of chaos that confronted them. Buildings, vehicles and aircraft were burning, while the tragic sight of death was unavoidable. They shakily made their way forward, with feet crunching on the debris that lay strewn around the base, and helped wherever they could. Personnel were running in all directions reacting to one emergency after another, as others sat, shaken and in shock. Huge holes had been ripped into the ground where bombs had fallen and to make matters worse a water main had been ruptured, which made the challenge of fighting the fires almost impossible. Despite all of this hardship, the defiance remained. People stoically cared for one another and immediately began taking steps to ensure that RAF Kenley would be back in the front line in the shortest time possible. Its relatively unprotected operations room had all of its communication lines severed, so the decision was taken to move to the butcher's shop in Caterham, which was being used as a training base for future operations staff.

Sunday, 18 August 1940 would go on to be known as 'The Hardest Day' as both the RAF and the Luftwaffe suffered its highest number of aircraft losses and the battle that raged represented the largest ever seen over Britain at that time. Attacks persisted all afternoon, with Victor and the remaining pilots of 'Treble One' being scrambled once again at 1700 hours to counter a raid that was attacking RAF Hornchurch and RAF North Weald. As the light faded, 111 Squadron had to count the cost of yet another momentous day of fighting. Two days after the loss of 'A' Flight's popular commander, Flight Lieutenant Ferriss, they now had to cope with the loss of 'B' Flight's ever-present leader, Flight Lieutenant Conners. Sergeants, Newton and Deacon, had been badly injured and were to spend many weeks in hospital before once again rejoining the squadron. Incredibly, the previous seven days of fighting had led to the death of seven pilots and a further five seriously injured. The heart of the squadron had been ripped out and the remaining pilots were noticeably feeling the strain. The rate of attrition of losing twelve pilots in one week was simply not sustainable and the decision was made to post 'Treble One' north of London to RAF Debden the following day.

In the space of three days both Victor and Kim had been caught on the ground and subjected to the unforgettable intensity and danger of German bombing raids. Their shared experiences and natural connection deepened as their blossoming friendship gained in importance. It offered both an escape and an exciting oasis in the otherwise chaotic and perilous world of warfare. Victor had spent a mere eighteen days with his new squadron but had experienced enough loss and upheaval to last him a lifetime. Ironically, despite his relative inexperience he was now in the group of pilots who were responsible for maintaining 'Treble One's' traditions and fighting verve as they waited for an influx of new members to arrive, often straight from operational training units. The following weeks would see Victor step into more of a leadership role but this brief respite to re-form would not last long. In a matter of days, the incredible demand exerted on Fighter Command meant that they had no choice but to call on 111 Squadron. Victor would find himself in the thick of the fighting once again, and all of this for a young man who eleven months ago was learning the art of flight in the sun-drenched skies over RAF Shoreham.

7

Attrition

The gruelling fight that erupted above Britain during the 'The Hardest Day' had taken its toll on both sides of the conflict and the pace of the battle noticeably slackened during the following few days. This relative lull allowed Fighter Command to reorganise its squadrons as best they could under the circumstances and send much-needed replacement pilots to those who had borne the brunt of the fighting. Often, these pilots would arrive directly from their training units with no combat experience and would be expected to join their squadrons and almost immediately go into battle. Over the next ten days, sergeants, Waghorn, Smythe, Page, Bumstead and Porter, all joined 111 Squadron but after seeing how raw these young recruits were Squadron Leader Thompson refused to use them operationally until they had gained some more flying time. The squadron then welcomed Pilot Officer Macinski and Flying Officer Kustrzynski, who had both seen service with the Polish air force during the Nazi invasion of their homeland in 1939. They had avoided capture and headed to England to carry on the fight but were still in the process of converting to the RAF's front-line aircraft. At a time when they were needed most of all, only one of these seven replacement pilots would go on to fly in combat for 'Treble One'. Any thought of supplementing the already depleted ranks with experienced pilots hadn't materialised, the only glimmer of hope was the return of Flying Officer Bruce, who had been given the rank of acting flight lieutenant and given command of 'B' Flight, and the arrival of Flying Officer Bowring from 600 Squadron.

Essentially, 111 Squadron had been bolstered in numbers only but the fighting strength of the squadron remained the same, if not weakened due to the ongoing fatigue of their operational pilots who were relied upon to take the strain.

Operating from RAF Debden, the squadron were immediately deployed on convoy patrols and were engaged in regular combat but the change in location and a very welcome change to the weather meant a momentary reprieve. Squadron Leader Thompson and Pilot Officer Walker both received a very well-earned Distinguished Flying Cross (DFC). The late Flight Lieutenant Conners was posthumously awarded the DFC with Bar. The only loss suffered by the squadron over the following week was that of Sergeant Sellars, who crash-landed and was injured after intense combat over a convoy on 26 August. Throughout this period, 'Treble One's' relentless pursuit of using the head-on attack remained, as time and again they surged into the midst of vast numbers of aircraft, sometimes in squadron strength but often only in threes or fours. It was proving to be such an extreme and costly tactic but these were extreme times and Squadron Leader Thompson knew no other way forward.

Almost as if they had drawn breath after an exhausting opening round, the Luftwaffe once again began sending huge formations across the Channel with the sole focus of attacking Fighter Command's bases and ending their resistance once and for all. The Luftwaffe seemed to have realised that only persistence would win this war of attrition and they were determined to pick up from where they left off. The intensity of the battle increased to new levels as it became clear that another Herculean effort would be needed to repel them. Victor was ready for that challenge. Something had shifted in his mindset since 18 August and he was displaying a real determination to get among the enemy. He had already been developing a reputation of being rock solid and totally dependable but now there was a very real edge to this sergeant pilot. Some of the other pilots of the squadron who had seen fighting during the Battle of France and now the early stages of the Battle of Britain were showing real signs of strain, some almost at breaking point, but something had switched within Victor. He'd taken the time to analyse the events of the previous three weeks and was ready to put some of his conclusions into action. No longer would he enter combat reacting to each situation in the air as it unfolded but he would be proactive, aggressive and decisive. Fighter Command was in desperate need of experienced pilots and despite his relatively limited time with the squadron, he had actually experienced a great deal and was ready to do his duty.

Saturday, 31 August dawned clear and fine and 111 Squadron had started the day in an all too familiar way – up at first light and arrived at dispersal ready for another day's action. They didn't have to wait long for the first call to scramble as by 0810 hours the nine available pilots of the squadron dashed to their waiting Hurricanes. The Luftwaffe had started the day by sending across a feint attack that actually comprised hundreds of Bf 109s in an attempt to lure British fighters into combat, but Air Vice Marshal Keith Park, 11 Group's now legendary commander, had seen it coming and did not react. What this feint did conceal, however, was a follow up raid of thirty Dornier Do 17 bombers escorted by at least forty Messerschmitt Bf 110s, which were heading straight for RAF Debden.

The nine Hurricanes of 'Treble One' clawed for height; the pilots searching the vast expanse of sky for their enemy. Victor was flying in yellow section with Pilot Officer Atkinson and Sergeant Silk as they swivelled their necks and squinted into the morning sun desperately trying to see the German aircraft. And then there they were. A vast gaggle of invaders stepped up in a large formation menacingly heading inland towards their base. Victor controlled the all-too-familiar pre-combat nerves that coursed through his body, and his mind began to settle into the task ahead. Yet again, the odds were far from favourable but his rapidly developing situational awareness summed up the scene in a matter of seconds – the bombers were the priority, they needed to be stopped and not the fighters. Almost as if he'd read his mind, the RT crackled into life and Flight Lieutenant Giddings gave his instructions to the squadron. He would lead his section of three aircraft in a head-on attack on the bombers and the remaining six aircraft would do their best to protect them from the forty German fighters. Once again, with gun buttons set to 'fire', 'Treble One' surged forward into battle as the sky erupted into a scene of chaos and the RT burst into life with warnings of aircraft coming in at all angles.

Out of the corner of his eye, Victor saw Flight Lieutenant Giddings and Flying Officer Bowring attacking the formation head-on with guns blazing as the Bf 110 escort moved into position to try and stop them. Cutting off their attack, the six remaining Hurricanes did what they could to keep these enemy machines at bay. Twisting and turning aircraft filled the sky as tracers from machine gun fire passed all too close to Victor's starboard wing tip and he pulled sharply away from the attack. A Bf 110 streaked in front of his windscreen in hot pursuit of another Hurricane and Victor reacted in an instant, opening up his eight Browning machine guns and pouring fire into the enemy machine. Parts of the Bf 110 were seen to fly off, leaving it no choice but to break off its attack and dive away to safety. A Dornier dived past billowing smoke from both engines before erupting into flames and falling earthwards. Victor hauled his aircraft around again and again, exerting a huge physical effort as he flew the Hurricane to its absolute limits. Vapour trails criss-crossed the morning sky as this intense dogfight raged and a parachute billowed open, drifting lazily earthwards. This belonged to Sergeant Craig, who had also been desperately trying to keep the Bf 110s at bay but had been shot down and baled out badly injured.

During the ensuing dogfight Flight Lieutenant Giddings claimed a Dornier 17 as destroyed, and a young South African pilot sergeant, Wallace, accounting for a Bf 110 and a probable Dornier 17. Flying Officer Bowring also found himself at the heart of the scrap, with a

Bf 110 reported as probably destroyed and further aircraft damaged. All nine pilots had thrown themselves into battle and were giving a very good account of themselves indeed but the adrenaline-fuelled intensity could not go on forever.

Hearing the hiss of compressed air signalling that he was now out of ammunition, with the fight still raging, Victor had no choice but to half-roll his Hurricane and dive steeply down to the decks. His air speed indicator picked up the pace as he glanced up and behind for any enemy machine that might have seen him dive away but the coast seemed clear. Down he went, holding the stick strongly as the forces picked up on the Hurricane and before long, he was flying low above the English countryside. He took a quick look around to get his bearings and then set course for base. The welcome sight of RAF Debden's satellite airfield, RAF Castle Camps, came into sight and he entered the circuit before landing. What a morning. As his Hurricane came to a stop and the ground crew got to work, Victor gratefully pulled off his flying helmet and basked in the cooling slipstream of the propeller. Despite their best efforts RAF Debden had been badly hit, with over 100 bombs falling on the base, but it remained operational.

Victor would be scrambled a further three times that day but as August 1940 drew to a close Fighter Command reflected on what had been a month of huge pressure as its airfields had been attacked regularly by day and bombs rained down on targets across Britain by night. Despite these relentless attacks, the squadrons of Fighter Command were standing firm but there remained great concern about the large number of pilots being lost and a very real lack of suitable replacements. If things carried on this way, then the battle of attrition would go down to the wire with so much being asked of these young men who had an average age of only 20 years old. Fatigue was starting to show on the faces of pilots from 'Treble One', with Squadron Leader Thompson sharing this telling insight:

I watched as one by one our aircraft returned to base after yet another sortie. Most aircraft to our delight had returned unscathed but then I saw a Hurricane coming in to land. His wings were tipping up, then down, then suddenly he hit the ground rather hard only to bounce right up again. Then at the second attempt he finally kept the aircraft on the ground and taxied a short way and stopped in the centre of the airfield. Casualty procedures were put into action and crash tenders and ambulances rushed towards him only to find the pilot fast asleep, he did not even have time to switch the engine off.

On 2 September 1940 the squadron were ordered to patrol Rochford at 15,000ft, where they sighted an enemy force of twenty Heinkel He 111 bombers protected by a large formation of Bf 109 and Bf 110 fighters. Once again Flight Lieutenant Giddings led the nine battle-weary pilots into a head-on attack and the now all too familiar melee of

The strain of battle is clearly evident on Victor's face after weeks of hard fighting.

Heinkel He-111 bomber.

aircraft intent on destruction filled the sky. A huge dogfight developed over the Thames Estuary as 'Treble One' tried desperately to keep the enemy machines from bombing their target. With body braced for action, Victor focused his attention on one of the Heinkels within the formation and got in a 'good burst', causing the aircraft's port engine to smoke profusely. The pleasure of seeing his bullets hit their mark was short-lived as out of nowhere a Bf 109 thundered in, shooting at Victor, leaving him no choice but to break off his attack and once again fly for his life. The two aircraft became separated from the main scrap as each pilot twisted and turned, trying to gain the upper hand in this deadly duel. As the seconds rolled into minutes, it soon became clear that through the prowess of his airmanship or by sheer determination Victor was gaining the upper hand. He managed to let loose another 'good burst' at his opponent, who was by now diving for cover and heading out to sea with the Hurricane in hot pursuit. The Bf 109 had a slight advantage in speed and streaked out low across the Channel with Victor unable to fire again but he maintained the chase and kept the pressure on his opponent before reluctantly peeling away and setting a course for base.

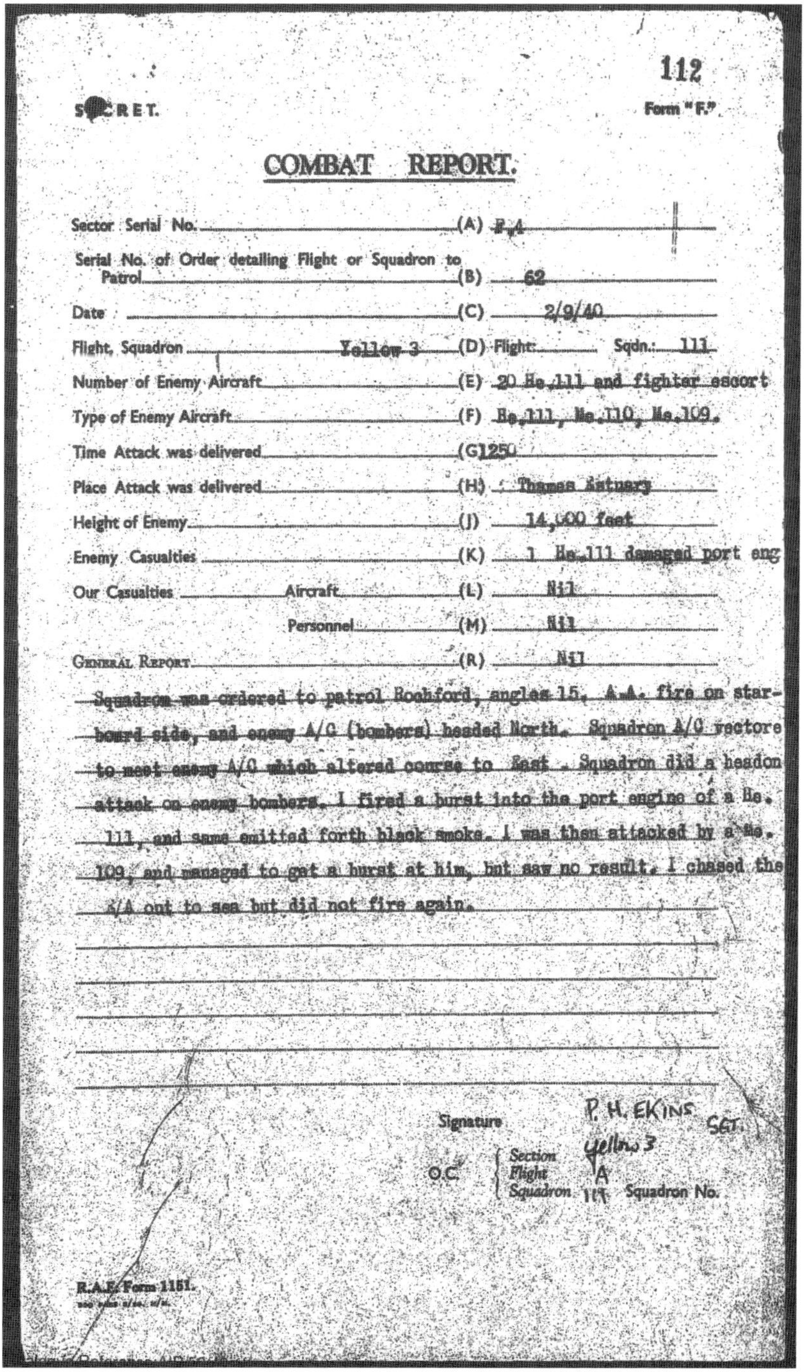

112

S●CRET.

Form "F."

COMBAT REPORT.

Sector Serial No. _____ (A) F.4

Serial No. of Order detailing Flight or Squadron to
Patrol _____ (B) 62

Date : _____ (C) 2/9/40

Flight, Squadron _____ Yellow 3 _____ (D) Flight: _____ Sqdn.: 111

Number of Enemy Aircraft _____ (E) 20 He.111 and fighter escort

Type of Enemy Aircraft _____ (F) He.111, Me.110, Me.109.

Time Attack was delivered _____ (G) 1250

Place Attack was delivered _____ (H) Thames Estuary

Height of Enemy _____ (J) 14,000 feet

Enemy Casualties _____ (K) 1 He.111 damaged port eng

Our Casualties _____ Aircraft _____ (L) Nil

_____ Personnel _____ (M) Nil

GENERAL REPORT. _____ (R) Nil

Squadron was ordered to patrol Rochford, angles 15. A.A. fire on starboard side, and enemy A/C (bombers) headed North. Squadron A/C vectored
to meet enemy A/C which altered course to East. Squadron did a headon
attack on enemy bombers. I fired a burst into the port engine of a He.
111, and same emitted forth black smoke. I was then attacked by a Me.
109, and managed to get a burst at him, but saw no result. I chased the
E/A out to sea but did not fire again.

Signature P. H. EKINS SGT.

O.C. {
Section Yellow 3
Flight A
Squadron 111 Squadron No.
}

R.A.F. Form 1151.

Victor's combat report from 2 September 1940.

Yet again, the combat that had taken place above the Thames Estuary that day had come at a cost. During his initial head-on attack, Flight Lieutenant Giddings' Hurricane had been badly hit and he was forced to make an emergency landing at RAF Detling just as the enemy raid flew overhead. He was able to crash land his aircraft successfully on the runway but he was caught in the middle of the attack as bombs fell all around, luckily being able to scramble for cover. Victor landed back at base to receive some devastating news that his friend and an ever-present member of 'A' Flight since he was first airborne with the squadron, a month ago to the day, Sergeant 'Bill' Dymond, was missing, presumed killed. 'Treble One' were not in a position to lose any more experienced pilots but yet again they counted the cost of battle and the pressure was about to intensify. The next day, they received the news that, due to the losses suffered by 85 Squadron, 111 Squadron were required to fly back to their former base at RAF Croydon to relieve them. They would once again find themselves in the heart of 11 Group and in the absolute epicentre of the fighting. The following days would be make or break for the squadron but the move had one consolation – Victor could once again see Kim.

On 4 September 1940 'Treble One' fell back into a routine that they knew all too well – up at dawn and fly down to their forward base of RAF Hawkinge. Victor had been rostered off flying duties for the day and was grateful for the opportunity to draw breath, as eight of the squadron's Hurricanes thundered south once again from RAF Croydon. A squadron at full strength consisted of twelve aircraft but this depleted force was all that 111 Squadron could muster. Within an hour of landing they were scrambled at 0900 hours to patrol Folkestone, in order to intercept a large raid that had been plotted heading across the Channel. Over seventy Heinkel He 111 bombers with a fighter escort of over 200 aircraft were flying in loose formation as high as 30,000ft. 'Treble One' were joined by two other squadrons from Fighter Command but once again faced daunting odds of around ten to one as Flight Lieutenant Giddings organised the squadron for another head-on attack. Ploughing into the enemy fighters, it was as if the whole German formation surrounded and then converged on the eight Hurricanes of 111 Squadron. Expertly manoeuvring his aircraft for the attack, Flight Lieutenant Giddings managed to shoot down two enemy machines in a matter of seconds before his aircraft was badly hit and spun out of control. Unable to carry on the fight, he made a forced landing at Catts Green Farm, Ewhurst, and was shaken but alive. It would prove to be his last combat involvement with the squadron and a huge loss for 'Treble One'.

The ensuing dogfight was a confused mass of aircraft that filled the sky, with burning fighters and bombers descending earthwards in all manner of directions. Under such extreme conditions, 111 Squadron had done an incredible job of keeping the aircraft at bay and managing to account for five destroyed enemy machines and many more damaged, but once again the price they had to pay was severe. Seconds after 'A' Flight's commander, Flight Lieutenant Giddings, had been hit, 'B' Flight's commander, Flight Lieutenant Bruce, had been tragically killed. Experience and leadership had been snatched away from 'Treble One' within days of the pair settling into the ways of the squadron. It was as if the dark days of August were repeating themselves once again. To make matters worse, the combat had been only the second flight for replacement pilot, Pilot Officer Macinski, who had also been shot down and was last seen crashing into the Channel. Poignantly, his death was recorded in the Operational Record Book of the squadron, on the same day that his posting to the squadron had been made official. Five shaken pilots would land back at RAF Croydon later that morning and Victor was immediately called upon to make up the numbers. He would go on to be scrambled three times throughout the day, with the squadron finally ending operations at an exhausting 2015 hours in the evening. It had been yet another exceedingly costly day for a squadron on the brink of collapse but they had no choice but to carry on and take the fight to the Luftwaffe. The freedom of the nation depended on it.

The pace of operations and the demands exerted on Fighter Command was absolutely relentless. The following day dawned clear and bright – perfect conditions for attack by the Luftwaffe. Once again, their target was RAF Biggin Hill and 111 Squadron were scrambled to intercept, managing to call upon the services of eight exhausted airmen. The previous day's combat had left them without any flight commanders, so the squadron reorganised into two sections of four aircraft and made the best of it. What transpired would stay with Victor for the rest of his life. Incredibly, and for one of the first times since he'd been with the squadron, 'Treble One' had managed to out-climb their opponent and were actually above the enemy formation when they were sighted. Added to this, they were able to position themselves with the sun behind them, giving them a huge tactical advantage as their position couldn't be identified by the invading force due to the glare. There they were, patrolling about 6 miles north of RAF Biggin Hill, eight Hurricanes looking down on an invading force of 120 aircraft.

All of a sudden, Flying Officer Walker, who was commanding 'B' Flight, was seen to dive away sharply. He'd experienced difficulty with his oxygen flow and, unbeknown to the rest of his flight, was diving to a lower altitude to regain normal breathing. Not knowing the circumstances, the remaining pilots of the section dutifully followed their commander down to the decks, unaware that he wasn't diving into combat. Incredibly, this left the four pilots of 'A' Flight to engage the enemy. Flying Officer Ben Bowring and sergeants, Ekins, Silk and Ritchie, facing odds of thirty to one, did the only thing that they knew how and that was to surge into the midst of this large enemy raid with guns blazing. As the four Hurricanes began their dive, they fanned out into a line abreast formation and, flying next to one another, hit a section of Dornier Do 17s from behind and above. Almost immediately Ben Bowring was hit by return fire and dived down, unable to regain control of his machine until he was at 5,000ft. This left the three sergeant pilots.

Victor had identified his target and was pouring machine gun fire into the enemy machine with devastating accuracy before being attacked by a number of Bf 109s. He was forced to break sharply and had no choice but to fly through the middle of this vast aerial armada with the German fighters in hot pursuit. Aircraft were all around and he instinctively ducked down in his cockpit as the threat of a mid-air collision seemed inevitable. Passing within inches, the sights of oil-stained engines, German gunners and the black Balkan crosses of the Luftwaffe ingrained into his mind, incredibly he emerged unscathed. The Bf 109s had followed Victor's dive and now a running dogfight ensued with each pilot fighting for his life. Fear gripped him as he hauled his aircraft around time and again flying it to its absolute limits, exerting so much force upon the Hurricane that he almost blacked out but somehow he continued to evade his opponents. Pure survival instinct forced him to keep swivelling his neck in search of attacks from behind as sweat poured from beneath his flying helmet and the monumental effort began to take its toll. Eventually he managed to get on the tail of one of the chasing Bf 109s and was able to get in two short accurate bursts, which he could see were hitting the mark. White smoke poured out of the enemy machine and it spiralled out of control heading earthwards before Victor was once again attacked from behind. Hauling his aircraft around in the tightest and most aggressive turn possible to avoid being hit, the blood was forced down from his head under the incredible G-force and he passed out. The sight of seeing the Hurricane dive steeply away out of control had the effect of convincing the German fighters that their quarry had been accounted for and they turned for home. In actual fact, Victor regained consciousness within a matter of seconds and, after regaining his composure, eased the Hurricane out of its dive.

The unforgettable events of this combat would stay with Victor throughout his entire life. Four brave young men had entered battle against daunting odds and somehow lived to tell the tale. Four Hurricanes flying side by side into the abyss. Sergeant Silk had been wounded in the forearm during the engagement, managing to crash land his damaged aircraft at Lullingstone Castle before being rushed to hospital. It was yet another loss to the depleted squadron but a small price to pay under these extreme circumstances. The following day would be no different. During combat on 6 September, Sergeant Tweed was seriously injured and Flying Officer Bowring, who had been temporarily placed in charge of 'A' Flight, had been injured in the arm and taken to hospital. 'Treble One' were on the brink of collapse.

The Luftwaffe had committed to this war of attrition with RAF airfields being their primary target and on 6 September 1940 the pressure was showing. Squadrons were being weakened by the day, suffering from a severe lack of suitable replacement pilots and with the infrastructure of the bases themselves in desperate need of repair. The defences of Fighter Command were battered but still intact and the question remained; how long could they hold out? Incredibly, an unlikely salvation was about to present itself. Winston Churchill had been angered by the bombing raid that Victor had witnessed on RAF Croydon on 15 August as it was the first time that innocent Londoners had suffered due to enemy bombing, despite Hitler's express orders not to attack the capital. On the night of 24/25 August bombs once again fell on London. In response, Churchill had ordered the first raid to be made on Berlin the following night, which incensed Hitler. Enraged by the British audacity in attacking the German capital, he began planning a new phase of the Battle of Britain and that was to send across the largest aerial formations ever seen and relentlessly bomb London into submission. A new threat was about to be unleashed on the British public and the depleted squadrons of Fighter Command would have to rise to this new and unexpected challenge, but their bases would get a vital reprieve.

111

SECRET.

R.A.F. Form 1151.

FORM "F"

COMBAT REPORT.

Sector Serial No. _____ (A) _____

Serial No. of Order detailing Flight or Squadron to
Patrol _____ (B) _____

Date _____ (C) 5th Sept. 1940

Flight, Squadron _____ (D) Flight "A" Sqdn. : 111

Number of Enemy Aircraft _____ (E) 50 Dorniers. 60 109's

Type of Enemy Aircraft _____ (F) _____

Time Attack was delivered _____ (G) 1015

Place Attack was delivered _____ (H) Near Biggin Hill.

Height of Enemy _____ (J) 15,000'

Enemy Casualties _____ (K) One ME 109 destroyed
(probable)

Our Casualties _____ Aircraft _____ (L) Nil

_____ Personnel _____ (M) Nil

GENERAL REPORT _____ (R) _____

P. 3 bursts of about 3 secs at
2/300 yards.

As Red 3 I took off with the Squadron having been ordered to patrol
at 15,000'. We climbed to 18,000' and saw enemy bombers approaching
from the South. Above them were ME 109's being engaged by Spitfires.
Red 1 led the section into an astern attack on a formation of 5
Dorniers, I got in a burst and was attacked by 109's. I broke away
and had a dog fight with a 109 chasing it S.E. I got 2 short bursts
at 15,000' and was attacked again from behind. The 109 I fired at
went down in a spiral dive emitting forth white smoke. I blacked out
and cannot pin point the position.

Signature Y.K._____ Sgt.

O.C. { Section Red 3
Flight A
Squadron   Squadron No. 111

(1611). W1.32346—2223. 400 Pads 12/38 T.S. 780

Catalogue Reference:AIR/50/43

Victor's combat report from 5 September 1940.

On 7 September 1940 Kim and the other WAAFs at RAF Kenley had been plotting the usual raid building up over France but something was different about this one. It was clear that this latest aerial armada was vast but nobody had expected what was appearing on the plotting table. The Luftwaffe had mustered an incredible 348 bombers that were being escorted by an unimaginable 617 fighters. It was the largest formation of aircraft ever seen, and it was creeping menacingly inland. As Fighter Command tried desperately to ascertain the tactics of the raid, working out which bases to protect, the formation just kept coming, like a formidable airborne battering ram. At 1642 hours the depleted remains of 111 Squadron were ordered to scramble and climb to 20,000ft. When the nine fatigued pilots broke through the cloud cover, they were in utter awe at the sight that confronted them. Never before had they seen such numbers as the sky was filled as far as the eye could see with aircraft. Like many of the squadrons from Fighter Command that were airborne, they did what they could but the magnitude of the raid had taken everyone by surprise, not to mention its intended target. 'Treble One' surged into the midst and made a head-on attack against some of the escorting Bf 110s. Victor was tucked in just behind Squadron Leader Thompson and both aircraft managed to get in telling bursts against the enemy but they couldn't hang around long enough to see the results of the attack. Another vicious scrap developed as each man flew his own individual battle for survival but the bulk of the enemy formation just carried on as if nothing had happened. As it approached the Docklands in London, the German bombers released their payload and set a course back for France. The damage caused was unimaginable.

That day, 7 September 1940, proved to be a huge turning point in the Battle of Britain and also for 111 Squadron. This change of tactic continued as huge formations of German bombers persisted in attacking London along with other major cities. The civilians who were once spectators to this epic battle that raged overhead were now very much on the front line as the nation as a whole began to bear

London ablaze after daylight attacks on 7 September 1940. Photo credit Andy Saunders.

the brunt of bombing. The result of the change of tactic from the Luftwaffe left thousands of Londoners dead and would eventually merge into what would become known as the Blitz. What this meant for Fighter Command, however, was some much-needed breathing space to repair its air bases and replenish its squadrons. The tactic of systematically knocking out the Royal Air Force as a precursor to invasion had been abandoned and now Germany was intent on bombing Britain into submission.

The reprieve that this had given Fighter Command had come too late for 111 Squadron. The unit had been utterly decimated and was no longer able to function as a front-line fighting force. Its remaining pilots were exhausted and the decision was taken by both Dowding and Park to remove them entirely from the battle and post them to RAF Drem in Scotland as a 'C' classification training squadron. It was a sad and sorry end to the Battle of Britain for a squadron that had given their absolute all in the quest for freedom. Since Victor's arrival just five weeks earlier, ten pilots had been killed in action, many of whom were irreplaceable flight commanders with precious combat experience. Many more had been seriously injured as time and again Victor had taken to the skies with friends, only to land and be forced to put their sudden loss out of his mind. It would prove to be the most intense period of his entire life.

Squadron Leader John Thompson's absolute conviction in using the head-on attack had been incredibly costly but he was a man that knew no other way. Always on the front foot and ready to join the fight, he persisted in using this extreme tactic for what he considered to be a very extreme situation, right until the end. It was incredibly successful in breaking up enemy formations and therefore could have potentially saved countless lives but in doing so it led to the death of many experienced pilots that simply could not be replaced and were needed now more than ever. A change was on the horizon for Victor but he would never forget those epic days during the Battle of Britain flying with 111 Squadron and would summarise his time with them in his usual understated way:

> It was a bit frightening because there were so many. A hundred bombers would come over escorted by 200 or 300 fighters. We were outnumbered by dozens, scores and we wondered how we were going to stop them. You came back to your room and there was an empty bed. You just put it to one side and carried on.

8

Looking for a Fight

Landing at RAF Drem on 8 September 1940 felt like landing in another world. Situated 20 miles east of Edinburgh and only a few miles away from the rugged coastline that was being battered by the North Sea, 111 Squadron were well out of harm's way. It led to a strange mix of emotions as the world of heightened existence that had been ever present for so long had been removed, literally overnight. A feeling of detachment was left as Victor knew only too well that the struggle for survival still raged down south and the pang to continue to do his duty was very real. There was also another pang – and that was for Kim. She had become such an ally to Victor during the previous weeks of fighting, as their joyous evenings and honest conversation had kept him in touch with all that was good in life. At a time when death and suffering were all around, his close friendship with her had represented hope, fun and as much as it was hard to consider under such circumstances – a future.

Despite these emotions, the breathing space that the squadron had gained by moving to Scotland was vital. Battle-weary pilots found their new quarters, stowed away their few belongings – and slept. Reoccurring images of burning aircraft and mortal combat invaded their dreams but at least they could begin the process of decompression. For Victor, this enforced break also gave him time and space for self-reflection. So much had occurred during the last five weeks that it took quite some thought to understand the level of self-development that had needed to take place in order to survive.

Where thirty-nine days ago a novice pilot once stood, eager to meet his squadron and join their elite ranks, now a battle-hardened veteran sat pondering life. He had found out that not only did he have the courage to overcome his fears about entering combat but he had been able to retain his presence of mind among the chaos and develop his skills. He hadn't overly considered what had been at stake but knew that he had a job to do and got on with it to the absolute best of his abilities. He had learned with immense speed during this baptism of fire and already he could sense the natural shoots of leadership rising from within. His generosity and modest, yet inspiring, personality had had a bonding effect on a squadron that was being torn apart. He'd developed a sixth sense and an awareness for others long before the war but it had been abundantly clear to those around him that his stoic and consistent manner were invaluable assets.

Photograph of 111 Squadron pilots taken shortly after they are posted to RAF Drem in Scotland. Left to Right. Pilot Officer Vykoukal, Flying Officer Walker, Pilot Officer Atkinson and Sergeant Ekins.

For now though, Victor had a job to do. He made his feelings known to Squadron Leader Thompson about the desire for an immediate move back down south to a front-line fighter squadron but 111 Squadron had been reclassified as a training squadron for inexperienced pilots and they were starting to arrive in their droves. After a few local practise flights to acclimatise himself with his new surroundings, Sergeant Victor Ekins was put to work. On 12 September 1940, and after just five weeks with 'Treble One', he led the squadron for the first time. It was quite a monumental moment being the lead aircraft with eleven other 'novice' pilots following his every word as they practised formation flying. The following day Victor was once again leading the squadron in a practise flight when they were vectored onto a potential enemy raid that had been plotted. Amazingly, as they climbed through the cloud, he spotted a lone Junkers Ju 88 but before they could engage the enemy machine dived into the cover of the cloud and headed back to base. During the next week, he would lead the squadron a further seven times, revelling in the trust and faith that Squadron Leader Thompson had put in him.

Over the previous few days there had been word coming from 11 Group, who covered the south-east of the country and therefore saw the vast majority of the fighting, that yet more pilots were needed to join front-line squadrons and Victor made sure that his name was top of the list. A new chapter was about to begin in his life and it really comes as no surprise as to where he was about to be posted – RAF Kenley. Whether by chance or the force of a quite determined personality, Victor was about to be reunited with Kim and join the iconic 501 'County of Gloucester' Squadron. They had proven themselves to be an elite collection of warriors who had been serving on the front line since the early days of the Battle of France. Full of tough and experienced characters, few other squadrons could boast the record that 501 Squadron had earned. Victor owed so much to his time with 'Treble One' and had witnessed such courage, bravery and an intense sense of duty. Now it was time to enter the fray once again, armed with these experiences and contribute as best he could to this huge struggle for freedom with his new squadron.

Arriving at RAF Kenley on 21 September 1940, Victor Ekins felt like he was home. After surveying the tattered remains of the hangars that had been destroyed on the 'The Hardest Day', he entered the mess and was greeted by the members of his new squadron, who marvelled at his 'magnificent moustache'. As with his first-day meeting 'Treble One', it would prove to be a whirlwind of introductions and conversations about the latest 'gen' but this time he was no outsider. An instant respect existed between him and the other young airmen, who knew only too well the perils of the career that they had each undertaken. They came across as a most likeable bunch with a terrific spirit, an undeniable competitive streak and an understated professionalism. Squadron Leader Hogan was clearly highly respected by his men and was regarded as a cool and

Hurricanes of 501 Squadron take off on a patrol from RAF Hawkinge.

efficient airman with a great shot. He had forged a squadron who had been battered but never beaten over the previous months of intense fighting, which he personified by sporting a quite impressive black eye sustained from baling out of his aircraft only three days earlier. Morale was high and it was such a welcome tonic for Victor after his turbulent experiences with 'Treble One'.

One man who made an immediate impression on Victor was the unforgettable Pilot Officer 'Bob' Dafforn. Standing at 6ft 7in tall, it took all his strength and acquired technique just to fit inside the cockpit of a Hurricane, let alone fly one in combat. They instantly hit it off. Bob Dafforn was a cheerful and engaging chap who came across as being completely dependable; he was definitely made of the right stuff. Another airman with whom he made an instant connection was Sergeant James 'Ginger' Lacey. Known to Victor as 'Jim', he had built quite a reputation for himself over the last few months of combat

Victor stands next to his good friend, Bob Dafforn.

and would go on to be one of the highest-scoring pilots of the Battle of Britain with eighteen confirmed victories. Sergeant Lacey had been a pre-war instructor and therefore a very experienced pilot indeed. He was a proud Yorkshireman with a direct yet relaxed manner and, in Victor's opinion, a great sense of humour. Despite being a little eccentric, he was without doubt an outstanding and ruthless fighter pilot straight from the top drawer.

One man who was unavoidable due to his vast personality was Sergeant Glowacki, who originated from Poland. Another rugged and tough individual who was full of fighting spirit after seeing the treatment of his homeland by the Nazis, 'Tony' Glowacki was always laughing. He was also a top pilot and a great shot, who had become an 'ace in a day' after shooting down five enemy machines in one day of combat on 24 August 1940. There seemed to be such strength in depth. Even the pilots who didn't make an immediate impression on Victor, like the quiet and meticulous Sergeant Paul Farnes, had built a reputation for being as tough as they came. After an evening of conversation, with pints of beer in hand, he had been made to feel most welcome and had been put in the picture as to the last few weeks of fighting in the south of the country. The Luftwaffe had continued to send across the vast formations that Victor had witnessed on 7 September and the losses on both sides had been mounting up. On 15 September, the Luftwaffe had taken a mauling at the hands of the squadrons from Fighter Command, yet still they came. During the few days before his arrival there had been a relative lull but London was still very much the target. Sergeant Victor Ekins was back on the front line, with a squadron that he could depend on, at a base that he knew well, where a certain member of the WAAF served as a 'plotter'. It was a fantastic posting.

On 23 September Victor took off on active operations with his new squadron for the first time. At full strength, the twelve aircraft of 501 Squadron were ordered to patrol Maidstone and then carry out a sweep over Dover but no enemy aircraft were sighted and they

501 Squadron based at RAF Kenley. Sitting on wing left to right: Sgt Morfill, Sgt Whitehouse, Sgt Pickering, Sgt Ekins, Sgt Laws. Middle row left to right: Sgt Grove, Sgt Holroyd, Sgt Gent, Sgt O'Byrne, Sgt Farnes, P/o Parkin, S/Ldr Hogan, F/lt Holden, P/o Dafforn, F/o Lee, F/o Jones, F/o Snell, P/o Witorzenc, P/o Don. Sitting front row left to right: Sgt Muchowski, Sgt Marcinkowski, Sgt Lonsdale, P/o Skalski, P/o Mackenzie, Sgt Lacey.

landed back at base at 1835. The following day they were up at dawn and airborne by 0825 hours to patrol London and the Thames Estuary. They could clearly see a formation of Bf 109s above flying at 15,000ft but the enemy didn't engage and the squadron kept a watchful eye on them before returning to base. It was a sign of the new tactics being employed by the Luftwaffe as large formations of fighters on 'nuisance raids' were being sent over but they didn't pack anywhere near the threat or punch of the bomber formations. The squadrons of Fighter Command knew full well that it was the bombers that they needed to stop, so were happy not to fall into the trap. These early days with 501 Squadron were rounded off with the usual evening gatherings, where Victor and 'Ginger' Lacey would spend many a happy hour in the company of Kim and fellow WAAF, Eileen Whiteman.

On the morning of 27 September 1940, it was clear from the outset that something big was building. It would prove to be another intense day of action along a huge front as the Luftwaffe once again tried to launch a serious assault on London. At 0855 hours the squadron responded to the call to 'scramble' and dashed to their waiting Hurricanes. In a matter of minutes, the twelve aircraft had formed up and were thundering into the sky above Kenley to intercept a large raid that had been plotted crossing the Channel. Despite its dangers, a feeling of exhilaration washed through Victor's body as once again he charged forth into battle. He was surrounded by a team of highly skilled warriors and the feeling of pride that he experienced seeing the squadron codes of SD and those unforgettable RAF roundels would stay with him forever. Together, 501 Squadron climbed for height and headed towards their course, which would take them south towards the coast and almost certainly to an enemy that was intent on destruction. Each pilot squinted into the morning sun and scanned the skies in search of the enemy machines. All of a sudden the call of 'bandits' crackled over the RT and in the distance, flying at 15,000ft, Victor could clearly see a formation of Heinkel He 111 bombers heading inland, high over the Kent countryside. With the distance between the two formations closing at a rapid rate, the pilots of 501 Squadron once again settled themselves in their cockpits for battle. Despite being one of the most experienced airmen on the squadron, Sergeant Lacey would never be able to control his leg involuntarily tapping as fear gripped his body, leaving him no choice but to remove it from the rudder bar of his aircraft before combat.

With ninety-six Browning machine guns roaring into life, the squadron singled out their individual targets and poured fire into the enemy machines. The Heinkels broke formation and seemed to spill out across the sky but within a moment were joined by the previously unseen Bf 110s that had been flying as fighter cover. A huge dogfight developed and Squadron Leader Hogan was able to get in a good burst before being forced to break off the attack as another Hurricane flew across his windscreen. Everything seemed to happen in an instant as Victor fired his guns at the enemy before almost immediately being attacked himself, forcing him to dive for cover. Pushing the stick forward violently, his Hurricane lunged earthwards and after swivelling his neck he was relieved to see that no enemy machine was on his tail. Pulling out of the dive, Victor found himself alone in what seemed like a completely empty sky. Without a second thought, he instantly pushed forward the throttle and climbed for all his worth in search of somebody to have a 'row with'. Whether it was the keenness of joining a new squadron or the relentless pursuit of combat that he had witnessed with 'Treble One', his mind was made up. Despite being completely alone and at a huge tactical disadvantage he wasn't about to give up just yet. Seeing nothing, he continued his climb through to 19,000ft, when out of nowhere he was set upon by three Bf 110s. They flew so close that he could clearly see the shark's teeth painted on the noses of the aircraft and the masked faces of the pilots.

Victor had been looking for a fight and now he'd found it. The enemy aircraft seemed to be attacking him from all angles and he felt alone, exposed and afraid. Twisting and turning with all of his might, he heaved the Hurricane about the sky desperately trying to evade his tormentors but they were gaining the upper hand. From behind, one of the Bf 110s began to pour fire into Victor's Hurricane. Without realising it at the time, a bullet hit him in the back, passed through his body and out of his stomach before smashing into the instrument panel and exploding. The Hurricane instantly caught fire and for a moment he sat there having been seriously injured, in a cockpit that was filling rapidly with flames. As the aircraft fell earthwards, instinct took over and he released the straps of the Sutton harness, disconnected his radio and oxygen supply, and slid back the canopy. Without any effort, he was sucked out of the burning Hurricane and started tumbling to earth. Grabbing the ripcord of his parachute, he gave it a sharp yank and was grateful when it billowed open, stopping his rate of descent with a sharp jolt. The carnage of the previous few seconds, as the wind had howled around his ears, was replaced by silence as he began drifting lazily earthwards. He found it to be quite a pleasant and peaceful experience. With adrenaline coursing through his body, he was still completely unaware of the severity of his wounds as the surreal tranquillity of the moment washed over him. This deep sense of peace was abruptly interrupted as he happened to look up and see his parachute peppered with bullet holes after being damaged in the attack. Luckily, it was able to take his weight and he started to search for suitable places to land.

From the ground, local residents watched in horror as the stricken Hurricane streaked across the sky, blazing like a torch and leaving a thick trail of black smoke in its wake. Victor's aircraft plunged earthwards, before exploding in a field among a sheet of orange flames. Villagers dashed towards it but were helpless spectators among a sea of debris as small fires burned far and wide. High above, three contented Bf 110 crews turned for base, pleased that their day's work had been completed successfully.

Bending his knees and bracing himself for impact, Victor returned gratefully to earth. As he pushed the parachute release button, which was located in his midriff, he was hit by an intense feeling of pain. Looking down, he saw his service uniform covered in blood and began to realise how badly he'd been hit. Incredibly, he'd landed next to a wooded area that was being used by a Canadian medical unit, who had watched him come down by parachute. In an instant a team of medics ripped open his clothing and began tending to his wounds. It was the most unimaginable stroke of fortune that almost certainly saved his life as his injuries were assessed and treated within minutes. Before he could really process what had occurred, he found himself in the back of an ambulance en route to Sevenoaks hospital. In his logbook he would simply write the words 'Engaged by 110s. Aircraft and self hit at 19,000 feet.'

Victor's time with 501 Squadron had lasted just six days and now he faced weeks of recovery as his wounds healed. He was left with a large scar on his back and an even larger scar where the exit wound had been, which would prove to be a permanent reminder of the epic events of 27 September 1940. While lying in his hospital bed in Sevenoaks, one emotion would not leave him and that was the shame he felt at being shot down. In some way he felt that he had let his new squadron down and a feeling of detachment once again fell over him. His mood was lifted by many visits from friends and family, who travelled down to see him from St Neots and, of course, visits from Kim. She was a mere 16 miles away and would make the journey to Victor as often as her shift pattern would allow. The days spent in hospital seemed to drag on and the nights were filled with the sound of air raid sirens and falling bombs as London was attacked relentlessly by the Luftwaffe. It was common practice for nurses to visit the ward and drag the beds away from windows in fear of broken glass and debris from falling bombs. He just wanted to be back with his squadron.

While Victor was in hospital the Battle of Britain officially ended on 31 October 1940. The squadrons of Fighter Command had stood firm in the face of huge pressure from the Luftwaffe and any thought of invasion had been abandoned due to the changed weather, tides and constant threat from the Royal Air Force. Hitler had never tasted defeat before as his forces had rampaged through Europe but the battle that had raged in the skies above Britain had brought that advance to an abrupt end. Five hundred and forty-four young RAF airmen had laid down their lives in this fight for freedom. Now the tactics used by the Luftwaffe were constant and devastating night attacks as major British cities were heavily bombed. The Blitz was now in full swing but the spirit of the people remained.

Incredibly, in under eight weeks Victor was declared fit enough to go back to his squadron and he could not wait to return to the fold. Travelling back to RAF Kenley, he rejoined 501 Squadron on 26 November 1940 and he was able to take his first flight in a Hurricane since being shot down. The weather had changed markedly since those long hot summer months and flying conditions were far from ideal. On 17 December he said farewell to his now beloved Kim as the squadron made the move back to their home base of RAF Filton, 7 miles from Bristol. By now their blossoming friendship had been cemented and they promised one another that they would stay in touch. Victor's last flight of 1940, only a year after he'd been taking his ab initio flight training, came on Christmas Day. With the squadron in high spirits and a delicious Christmas dinner eaten, the CO decided to punish his men for drinking too much by ordering a battle climb. In squadron strength they climbed to, as 'Ginger' Lacey

would record in his logbook, '30,000 frozen feet'. And so ended the most intense year of Victor's entire life. On Sunday, 29 December 1940, he sat down and laid a small, blue 'Service Diary' in front of him. He felt compelled to write and would go on writing every single day throughout the rest of the war. Poignantly the first word written in his diary was 'Kim'.

Victor enjoys some solitude as he sits down to write.

9

Jerry a Nuisance

At RAF Filton the pilots of 501 Squadron experienced a very different pace of life compared to the intense and relentless summer days of the Battle of Britain. Due to the poor weather and unfavourable flying conditions, there was very little urgency in squadron activity. Pilots were able to take some long overdue leave and Fighter Command used the time to reorganise its squadrons in preparation for the next phase of the conflict. The change in tempo eased the burden that the pilots had so recently carried and they settled into life in the West Country with ease. Victor was able to travel back to St Neots with Kim and introduce her to his parents during a lunch date at the Bridge Hotel. After this dutiful interlude the pair made their way to the Bonnington Hotel in London to see in the New Year by attending a party at the popular London nightspot the Coconut Grove that lasted until 0430 hours. After a very necessary late start the following day, they met up once again and went to the pictures to see *The Thief of Bagdad*. All of this to the backdrop of falling bombs and air raid sirens, such was the soundtrack to young love during the Blitz.

Victor returned to Filton on 2 January and was rostered onto night flying duties the following night. The German High Command had broadened the reach of its Blitz campaign over Britain and now more and more cities were being viciously bombed at night in an attempt to force Britain to surrender. Targets such as Cardiff, Bristol, Plymouth, Portsmouth and Coventry were all dealt destructive blows and being based at Filton meant that 501 Squadron were tasked with the job of countering this menace. The Royal Air Force had no purpose-built, radar-equipped night fighters at this time so the fighter boys in their Hurricanes were expected to get airborne and do what they could. It was a frustrating task.

Night flying was a very different pursuit compared to the almost instinctive endeavours of the dogfight. Gone was the ability to check outside the aircraft for landmarks, to fully focus on catching your quarry and to feel the freedom of pure aviation. In its place was the lonely, intense and draining process of flying your aircraft solely by its instruments. Fighting off all fears, urges and instincts, knowing that only your full focus and faith in those dials on the instrument panel would keep you alive. On 3 January 1941, Victor surged into the snow-filled skies above RAF Chalmey Down and into a very uncertain night. He soon began to feel the hopelessness of the situation as he roamed around in search of the enemy machines, as the cities beneath him blazed. In the cramped, unheated and freezing cockpit of the Hurricane, it was almost impossible to see beyond the glare of the Rolls-Royce Merlin exhaust stubs, let alone through the cloud and snow, but that didn't stop Fighter Command demanding that their pilots give it their all. Anger and frustration boiled up in Victor as he spent one hour and forty-five isolated minutes roaming the skies but being completely helpless to stop the damage being caused below. At 0145 hours he lowered down into the circuit and gratefully felt the airfield rise up to meet the wheels of his undercarriage – he was exhausted. Victor would merely note in his most understated way 'Jerry a Nuisance'.

Throughout the entire month of January, weather seriously hampered both the German attacks and RAF defence. Snow, fog and sub-zero temperatures fell on RAF Filton and the pilots of 501 breathed a sigh of relief when they received orders that night flying was cancelled for the evening due to the conditions. Invariably, this led to many impromptu nights out with his new squadron as the natural ability that Victor had to make meaningful connections flourished. Whether he was playing cards with 'Ginger' Lacey or out at The Railway pub with Morfill, Whitehouse, McKenzie and Dafforn, Victor truly began to feel part of the brotherhood of 501 Squadron. It was a novel feeling to be able to leave the intensity and fatigue of the previous year behind momentarily and exist within this relative calm. On 15 January Sergeant James Lacey was deservedly promoted to pilot officer and given a fortnight's leave. His home town of Wetherby was expecting him and was lying in wait with a hero's welcome, but this celebration had to be put on hold for a few days as once again 'Jim' and Victor headed to London to see Eileen and Kim. They spent three blissful evenings dancing into the early hours at the Davis Club at Croydon before 'Jim' eventually made the journey home. Throughout the remainder of the month the awful weather and flying conditions remained, limiting Victor to only eleven flights for the squadron. Tragedy also struck 501 Squadron as

The brotherhood of 501 Squadron. 'Ginger' Lacey, 'Mac' McKenzie, Tony Whitehouse, Bob Dafforn and Victor Ekins.

Victor, Kim, 'Ginger' Lacey and Eileen Whiteman.

Sergeant Gent was killed in a flying accident while ferrying a Miles Magister to RAF Filton.

As the weeks went by and conditions began to improve, so too did the energy and drive surrounding the squadron. Despite the pilots being grateful for the reprieve that had accompanied the winter months, they were now chomping at the bit to get at the enemy. Fighter Command began to prepare its squadrons for the demands that surely lay ahead and for 501 Squadron that meant a period of transition. Many of the pilots who had seen combat since the early days of the Battle of France were either posted to new squadrons or to operational training units to spend time as an instructor and away from the front line. They were in desperate need of a rest from combat and 501 squadron began to welcome a host of new pilots to its ranks. By now Victor was fast becoming an established member and was thrilled when, on 9 February, Flight Lieutenant Morello took him to one side and spoke for the first time about a permanent commission to the Royal Air Force. Until now, the route that he'd taken through the VR had seen him on temporary commission as a sergeant pilot but his natural leadership abilities and solid airmanship had been plain for everybody to see. To further this feeling of recognition, Victor led 'B' Flight on a formation flight on 19 February, being the lead aircraft ahead of some of the squadron's most experienced fliers.

Tony Whitehouse and Victor sitting on the wings of a Hurricane with Bob Dafforn in the cockpit.

On 22 February 1941, the pilots sat at RAF Filton as once again the snow began to fall. Flying conditions were far from favourable but their revelry in the dispersal hut had been interrupted by the sound of an enemy raider that briefly roamed around in the clouds above. Each pilot shrank a little in his seat knowing that soon Fighter Command would call and ask for a section to intervene and they were loath to leave the comfort of their chairs and their place around the warm fire. Victor had just arrived at dispersal sporting a fresh haircut and had a nasty feeling that he would be chosen. Each airman looked on pensively as the phone repeatedly rang, until, sure enough, Fighter Command asked if 501 Squadron could get two Hurricanes airborne to do what they could. The snow had become heavier with a cloud base down to 1,000ft and Pilot Officer McKenzie boldly put his name forward for the job. Scanning the dispersal hut, he caught sight of the freshly shaven and sharp-looking Victor and promptly volunteered his services as his number two.

Climbing into their Hurricanes and taxiing out to the runway, it very much had the feeling of a forlorn mission. The visibility was terrible and as the aircraft clawed for height they were almost immediately engulfed by thick cloud and snow. Keeping station on 'Mac's' wing tip, it took all of Victor's concentration not to lose or collide with his leader. Large pieces of snow passed almost horizontally across his windscreen as the pair stooged around the murk in search of their elusive foe, which the ground controller had reported as a He 111. They flew a course between Bristol and Filton looking for the nuisance raider but with visibility now getting dangerously low and the chance of landing safely back at base diminishing by the minute, the pair were ready to call time on the search. The voice of the controller crackled faintly over the RT and gave new orders to travel down to Avonmouth docks. As 'Mac' and Victor began a gentle turn they became aware of a swirling hole in the mist, which for a split second looked like it had a shadowy shape in the middle of it. They flew towards the tunnel that had been created among the murk but as they approached, the mist once again engulfed them and the moment almost instantly passed. They continued the search but before long any thought of pursuing the enemy raider had become secondary as both pilots struggled desperately with the conditions and were incredibly relieved when the cloud parted momentarily to reveal the welcome sight of RAF Filton below. The pair entered the circuit and were extremely grateful for the dull thud as their Hurricanes returned to earth.

Later that afternoon, and having retaken their snug positions in the dispersal hut, the phone rang and the adjutant proudly reported that the crew of a Heinkel bomber had been taken prisoner after their aircraft had crash-landed at Avonmouth docks. The aircraft had incredibly been brought down by a single gunner on a moored ship using a Browning machine gun. After interrogation, however, the crew of the German aircraft revealed that their flight in the relative safety of the clouds had been rudely and quite surprisingly interrupted by the sight of two Hurricane fighters. The pilot of the bomber had thrown the aircraft into a dive and made for the Bristol Channel, where it was subsequently shot down. Victor and 'Mac' were very pleased that their afternoon's work was not totally in vain, and both tried to claim one enemy aircraft as 'scared' when they reported the incident to the intelligence officer. Their claim was denied.

During March 1941 the squadron continued to experience much change. Flying constant patrols and covering naval convoys, the more experienced pilots were tasked with getting the newcomers up to speed with the ways of the squadron. On multiple occasions Victor would be trusted with leading a section of two new sergeant pilots as they became accustomed to both the Hurricane and the local area. He was stepping into the world of leadership and was completely at ease with the transition. There was also a growing dynamism within Fighter Command during this period as discussions between top brass took place about what tactics should be employed moving forward. The Luftwaffe were still pummelling Britain by night but the intense, large-scale daylight raids had yet to rematerialise despite weather conditions starting to improve. Passively waiting to be attacked and fighting another defensive war of attrition didn't seem like a favourable option, so plans were formulated about how the Royal Air Force could go on the offensive. No. 501 Squadron were ready. They were fast becoming rejuvenated in terms of fresh pilots and the bond within the squadron was constantly being reinforced with games of 'rugger' and regular trips to Bristol. Victor worked hard by day and lived the life of a normal 26-year-old by night, enjoying parties and celebrations with his 'boys'.

His relationship with Kim was also flourishing and the pair were in almost daily contact. Whether they were chatting on the telephone in the evenings or writing and receiving letters, it was clear that their love for one another was special. They were to meet once again in a snow-covered London on 1 April 1941 and enjoy going to the 'flicks' and dancing into the night. Victor had been sent to London to

Victor sitting at the feet of Bob Dafforn, alongside Tony Whitehouse and an unknown member of 501 Squadron.

Above: Tony Whitehouse, Bob Dafforn and Victor.

Right: Tony Whitehouse, Bob Dafforn and Victor.

attend an interview at Adastral House the following day to confirm his commission to the Royal Air Force. On 7 April he was officially promoted to pilot officer and was able to share the news with his family in person while on leave to collect his new uniform from Bedford. He spent some much-needed quality time with loved ones, attending church with his mother and sister, Cynthia, before enjoying a round of golf at St Neots golf course with his father. On 12 April 1941, he returned to his squadron ready to get down to business at their new base of RAF Colerne. The squadron had moved from RAF Filton so that they could make up part of the Tangmere Wing and take part in Churchill's programme to strike back at the Nazis. They were about to go on the offensive.

The RAF had learned many lessons from the epic events of 1940, witnessing Hitler's forces being constantly on the front foot as they rampaged their way across Europe. They had never really tasted defeat or been stopped until the natural barrier of the Channel had forced them to reconsider their tactics and attack Britain by air as a precursor to invasion. Despite this enforced change, they still held a lot of the tactical cards that came with offensive operations. They chose their targets, what time they were to be attacked, how high they would be attacked from, how many aircraft would be deployed and which squadrons they would use. Where possible they would use the weather conditions to their advantage and make sure that their pilots could attack with the sun behind them in order to restrict the visibility of the defenders.

The pilots of Fighter Command had no choice but to wake each morning before dawn and wait at a state of 'readiness' for the enemy to come. The days would prove to be long and exhausting, with hours on end spent battling the nerves, waiting for the phone to ring to get them airborne. They would spend long periods of time completely inactive interspersed with short, sharp, intense and potentially deadly activity. Victor would go on to describe the Battle of Britain as 'exciting, frightening, arduous and dull'. Always climbing to meet the enemy, which put them at a huge tactical disadvantage and heavily outnumbered, they were the first fighting force in the world to stop Hitler in his tracks. The biggest advantage that the RAF had fighting over home soil was that any airman who took to his parachute could immediately rejoin their squadron, whereas members of the Luftwaffe became prisoners of war. As spring 1941 started to blossom, the tables were about to turn.

The Royal Air Force would no longer wait to be attacked under these conditions but began the process of taking the fight to Germany. Surprised by the fact that Hitler hadn't reignited his campaign to invade Britain, it began identifying targets of military importance that could be reached by its pilots and crews. It would mean co-operation between both Fighter and Bomber commands, and a new chapter in the war. On 17 April 1941, 501 Squadron flew as part of the Tangmere Wing to escort eighteen Bristol Blenheims on a bombing raid on Boulogne docks. Victor had woken that morning feeling pretty awful and was hugely disappointed when the 'doc' had told him that he couldn't fly. Flight Lieutenant Cam Malfoy led the squadron on a two-hour sortie over occupied Europe as the Blenheims battled through heavy flak to bomb their target. It had taken the German fighter defences completely by surprise and had made a definite statement to Hitler. In reality, the relatively light Blenheim bombers made little impact on their target and the hundreds of fighters that had escorted them was massive overkill for a raid of that size but it was a start. There would be ample opportunity over the coming years to learn these lessons and perfect the process of aerial bombing but it represented a huge step forward.

10

On the Offensive

The decision to take the fight to Germany led to a renewed vigour and drive that swept through Fighter Command. It also signalled more changes for 501 Squadron, not least the fact that they were about to receive an influx of 'new' aircraft. The raid over Boulogne would prove to be the end of an era as it was the last full-scale mission that the squadron undertook flying the Hurricane. This rugged and tough aircraft that had been an ever-present ally since the Battle of France was about to be replaced by the Supermarine Spitfire Is recently vacated by 66 Squadron. Adored by those who flew it, pilots would comment that you didn't get into a Spitfire, you strapped it on. It could turn tighter, climb higher and was incredibly manoeuvrable. Being powered by the same Rolls-Royce Merlin engine gave it an air of familiarity but the change represented a huge upgrade for the squadron. It seemed as though Hitler had momentarily taken his eye off Britain and Fighter Command were making the most of it. The 24 April 1941 would go down as an important day in the squadron's history as its pilots were proudly presented to the Queen Mother during a visit to RAF Colerne and the first of the new aircraft arrived at base.

Five days later, Victor took to the skies in Spitfire R6837 for his first flight as he 'gained experience on type'. Throwing the aircraft around the sunny skies above RAF Colerne for thirty minutes was an incredible thrill. He celebrated this momentous day by playing the piano for an hour, much to the joy of the rest of his squadron, who liked nothing more than a beer-fuelled sing-song. These were memorable times for the pilots of 501 Squadron, who were in buoyant mood. The dark intensity of the previous year was by now well out of their system and with fresh blood, new machines and positive new tactics, there was plenty to look forward to. Another memorable day arrived shortly after as Victor welcomed two new pilots who had recently arrived from 55 OTU. Pilot officers, Robin Wheldon and Anthony Palmer-Tomkinson, had trained together and would become firm friends of Victor's over the coming months. A keen sportsman and talented skier, Palmer-Tomkinson or 'PT' as he was known to the squadron, was a 'gentle and kind man' with a huge personality. He came from a family of incredibly high standing in British society who were directly related to the Royal Family. Despite being only 20 years old, 'PT' made an instant impression on the squadron with his upbeat attitude and keenness to get at the enemy. Victor connected with Robin on another level and he soon became known as the intellectual of 501 Squadron. Being slightly older at 25 years and having been educated at Oxford, gaining an Honours Degree in History, Robin Wheldon had a wise head on young shoulders. He had grown up in a household dominated by the legal profession and this had shaped him into someone who was more comfortable witnessing and observing rather than being the centre of attention. He and Victor instantly clicked and the three pilots would go on to forge a brotherly bond, both in the skies above France and the many night spots that the trio would visit after a hard day of operational flying.

The intensity around the squadron noticeably increased in April and May 1941 with constant fighter patrols, convoy patrols and squadron formation flying. Although it was still rare to engage any enemy aircraft in combat at this time, there was a very real need to prepare the squadron's pilots for offensive operations in the Spitfire. Flying an aircraft during combat meant knowing it inside and out, and being confident enough in your machine to fly it to its absolute limits. With the influx of new pilots and many of the existing members

Left: Victor alongside Robin Wheldon.

Below: A young Anthony Palmer-Tomkinson.

still getting to know their new steed, the squadron became extremely active. On 11 May, Victor along with Flight Lieutenant Cridland and Sergeant Holroyd, was up at dawn and airborne by 0410 hours on a morning fighter patrol. After forty uneventful minutes roaming the skies above Britain in search of enemy reconnaissance aircraft, the three pilots landed and were able to have a brief chat with sergeants Smithers and Crozier, who were about to get airborne for a convoy patrol. After sighting the convoy, the pair started practising evasive tactics and, for no apparent reason, Smithers was seen to lose control of his aircraft and was tragically lost in the sea. News of the event reverberated around the squadron but they were airborne once again later the same day in squadron strength for what Victor describes as a 'flap'. His day's work would not finish until the following morning at 0400 hours after being on night readiness, meaning Victor was either at readiness or airborne for a twenty-four-hour period.

The routine of night flying, offensive fighter patrols and convoy patrols persisted as the squadron became one with its new aircraft and, due to a reshuffle in personnel, truly began to take shape. In June, Squadron Leader Gus Holden was promoted and replaced by Squadron Leader Adrian Boyd, who joined the squadron with boundless energy and enthusiasm to get at the enemy. 'Ginger' Lacey was promoted to flight lieutenant and given 'A' Flight, while 'B' Flight was placed in the gifted hands of Flight Lieutenant Bob Dafforn. By now Victor was an integral and established member of the squadron who would regularly lead 'B' Flight in Dafforn's absence. It had been an intense and productive few months of activity but Victor was grateful to be able to take six days leave and travel with 'Jim' to Torquay, where the pair met Eileen and Kim, heading straight out to the pub. The foursome then paired off as Victor and Kim spent some much-needed time together as their relationship deepened. They went ice skating, visited a spa and spent the day at the local tourist attraction Smugglers Cove. Each day was, of course, concluded with a night of dinner and dance that more often than not ended at 0300 hours. On his return to

'Ginger' Lacey writes a personal note to Victor.

RAF Colerne the following day, the couple would then speak on the telephone at 1830 hours, 2030 hours and midnight, with Victor writing a letter to his dearest before eventually drifting off.

On 22 June 1941 Victor would scribe the words 'RUSSIA INVADED' into his diary. These were two simple words that had huge implications. Germany had inexplicably turned its back on Britain and made an all-out assault on their 'natural enemy' to the East. In doing so it had started a war on two fronts and, despite the damage caused to Britain the previous year, had abandoned any attempts to invade. Fighter Command had questioned why 1941 had started so slowly and had gratefully used the time to prepare and reorganise its squadrons – now it knew the reason. Hitler had strategically moved the majority of his land forces to the East. Up until this point the two nations had been allies, had signed the Nazi-Soviet Pact and invaded Poland together in 1939, sharing out the spoils of war between them. In an instant that had all changed. For the next three weeks 501 Squadron were to endure more frustrating night flights from RAF Chilbolton but the tide was turning and everybody could feel it. Now it was imperative that Russia were supported in any way possible and this opportunity not lost.

On 8 July, Victor's logbook would simply note that himself and Pilot Officer Robin Wheldon had taken a flight in the squadron's

Miles Magister T9747 to RAF Wyton. In actual fact, the pair had bent protocol somewhat and flown to Victor's home town of St Neots, with his diary noting that they had 'landed on the Common'. This was an open expanse of common land conveniently situated a few hundred metres away from the Ekins family home. Victor then went on to pick Kim up from Bedford and spend a few welcome days with loved ones, away from night flying. They visited both The White Horse Pub and The New Inn, and he was able to share an evening with his father. It was a visit that very much had the feeling of the calm before the storm as only a few days later he was on the offensive.

On the evening of 13 July 1941, the squadron gathered as one to attend a briefing about the following day's raid. The briefing room was consumed with the buoyant atmosphere of the pilots as conversation and speculation drifted back and forth. The smoke-filled room reverberated with the sound of shuffling chairs and voices until the commanding officers walked in, gaining the attention of the men. They stood at the front of the room, addressing the pilots, and did their best job of making a rousing speech about 'taking the fight to the enemy'. It was packed full of cliché but was well intended and appreciated by all. Then, the moment of truth came as they revealed a large map of the south of England and mainland Europe that was covered in red string all leading to one destination: Cherbourg. No. 501 Squadron were to provide high cover for a formation of Blenheims, with Victor put in charge of 'B' Flight in the absence of Bob Dafforn, who was on leave. His formation included pilot officers, Wheldon, Palmer-Tomkinson, Newbury, Raba and Sergeant Holroyd. With watches synchronised and as much intelligence consumed as humanly possible, Victor felt ready. He went to bed early that night mindful of the dawn start and full of thought about the following day's mission.

As the squadron surfaced the following morning and emerged through the lethargy of the early hours, it was down to business.

Victor had experienced many offensive fighter patrols where a group of aircraft would fly up and down the Channel in sight of the French coast but this would be the first time that he would penetrate European airspace and fly over Nazi-occupied land. The nerves were present, of course, and he actively kept at bay any thought of being shot down and captured over enemy territory, which was now a very real possibility. The skills that he'd learned many years ago at Bishop's Stortford College of keeping his emotions in check became a vital ally and the energy he gave off to those around him was of a calm, solid and dependable leader. The twelve aircraft of 501 Squadron took off from RAF Chilbolton and made their way to RAF Warmwell, where they were to rendezvous with the rest of the formation.

At 0730 hours, with the rest of the aerial armada in place, they headed off as one into uncertain skies towards Cherbourg. Victor couldn't deny the sense of feeling exposed as England disappeared from view behind them and the formation was confronted with the quite daunting prospect of flying over the vast expanse of water that lay between them and their target. The Channel looked so innocent, almost enticing, but Victor knew that it would engulf himself and his aircraft in an instant given the chance. They were leaving safety behind, with danger ever present below and heading into the unknown. Regardless of these challenges, there was also a huge sense of pride as if they were on a crusade to free Europe of Nazi tyranny. A sky full of Allied aircraft and airmen, forming a single, unstoppable fighting force. The formation carried on relentlessly to its target. Flying top cover gave 501 Squadron an element of freedom compared to those who were detailed with either escort cover or, even worse in Victor's opinion, close cover. Yet the whole process still went against all of the instincts of the fighter pilot, who had always been told to never fly straight and level in the combat zone for more than twenty seconds. Their job now was to protect the bombers at all costs.

As the French coast appeared ahead, Victor found that he had settled into the flight. Being the lead aircraft in a formation of six seemed to keep his mind focused and he alternated between searching the skies for enemy fighters and keeping a sharp lookout on his men. The sun beamed in through the canopy and the ever-present hum of the Rolls-Royce Merlin ahead gave comfort and confidence. Almost anticlimactically they crossed the coast and were now flying over enemy territory when all of a sudden innocent looking black puffs started to appear all around. The German defenders had put up one of their notoriously accurate 'flak' barrages and the whole formation seemed to be surrounded by anti-aircraft fire. Initially the experience was quite intriguing until one exploded dangerously close and within the dark cloud lurked a fiery red, devilish core. Victor's Spitfire was rocked by the explosion but carried on unperturbed and he marvelled at the resilience and fortitude of the bomber pilots below, who flew on as if nothing had happened.

By now the formation was over Cherbourg and the bombers flew straight and level as they began their bombing run. A call over the RT declared 'Bandits, twelve o'clock high, coming down now' and, looking up, Victor could see a line of Bf 109s surging towards their formation. A section was detailed to break away and face the attack, which flared up in an instant, but the pilots of 501 Squadron were joined by another squadron and the threat was countered, with one Bf 109 damaged and another destroyed. Below the bombers released their bombs and Victor could clearly see the clouds that the explosions created. Onwards the formation went, still straight and level, with each and every pilot willing the lead bomber to start his turn for home. Eventually, turning slowly to port, the whole armada manoeuvred as one and began to set course for England. This represented one of the most dangerous parts of the mission for the fighter pilots as those flying on the outer edge of the turn were seriously exposed and vulnerable to attack. It proved to be an immense test of nerve to hold course and direction knowing that at any moment you could be attacked with the potential of your day ending in a German prisoner of war camp – or worse. All 501 Squadron could do was keep constant visual and exert maximum concentration; it was a mentally draining affair.

With the target now behind them, the formation set course for England. Flying through another flak barrage and keeping a close eye on a group of enemy fighters flying above but had not yet attacked. They started to make progress until they were once again across the French coast and out over the vast expanse of sea. With the promise of England ahead, Victor's mind wandered momentarily to thoughts of Kim, home and safety but he checked them as soon as they appeared and he refocused on the job in hand. It wasn't time to be complacent. He drew strength from those around him and they from him. He was doing his duty to the nation, of course, but almost more important was the thought of not letting his squadron down. Of giving the best of himself and keeping his men safe. It was impossible to replicate this sense of belonging as each man existed within the almost unbreakable brotherhood of the squadron.

In the distance Victor clearly made out the sight of the English coast line – and what a sight it was. The formation began to lose height as it approached the coast and before long 501 Squadron peeled away from their position of top cover and headed back to base. They landed at 1150 hours that morning and Victor taxied gratefully back to dispersal to be met by his ever-present ground crew. It had been a successful but mentally draining flight. Tellingly, that evening there was no trip to the pub or boisterous night out, only a letter to Kim and an early night. The concentration and intensity of the day had taken its toll, and it was only the beginning.

The following week after the first Cherbourg raid, 501 Squadron were detailed with practise formation flights with an ungainly 30-gallon long-range fuel tank under their wings. The process was hated by the pilots as their aircraft lost all of their natural manoeuvrability, especially in the turn, which became awfully slow. It was a huge relief when the order came over the RT to 'drop tanks' and the Spitfire leapt with joy after shedding this restrictive load. Speculation was rife

'Ginger' Lacey being presented with a scarf in recognition for shooting down the Heinkel He 111 that bombed Buckingham Palace on 13 September 1940.

Victor makes sure that 'Ginger' is looking the part.

501 Squadron pilots gather as 'Ginger' climbs into the cockpit of his Spitfire. Victor is standing centre shot, next to Anthony Palmer- Tomkinson.

between the men as to why they were undertaking such training and, more importantly, which far-flung destination they would be asked to attack. They wouldn't have to wait long to find out. A target of the highest priority for the RAF at this time were the German battleships *Scharnhorst* and *Gneisenau*, which had been moored in Brest harbour. They were the absolute pride of the navy and the German High Command were desperate to release them from their mooring and get them actively into the war once again but they were hemmed in both by sea and air. No. 501 Squadron were training for the role of 'top cover' but this time they would be flying to the edge of the Spitfire's range and beyond. A briefing on the night of 23 July would detail a flight that would cover a 150-mile expanse of water before bombing Brest Harbour. It was defended by one of the heaviest flak belts in Europe and had a German fighter squadron based nearby. All of this combined with the unnatural drop tanks needed to make up the extra range left each man present at the briefing in no doubt – this would be tough. Victor would take up his usual position in 'B' Flight alongside his leader, Flight Lieutenant Dafforn, and pilot officers Raba, Wheldon, Holroyd and Palmer-Tomkinson.

The outward leg of the journey to Brest seemed to last an eternity. Fourteen aircraft from 501 Squadron had joined with ten more from another squadron to form the top cover. They had flown to RAF Predannack, the most westerly of the bases, to top up with fuel before embarking on their 150-mile epic. Keeping revs at a steady rate and cruising at 15,000ft, Victor once again marvelled at the spectacle of the Royal Air Force on the offensive. The sky around and below him was full of purposeful aircraft bearing the iconic RAF roundel, all heading forth as one. As he looked across to the rest of the squadron, he could clearly make out the large frame of Bob Dafforn filling the cockpit of his Spitfire and Anthony Palmer-Tomkinson seemingly deep in concentration. These were his teammates, his family, and it filled him with the most incredible sense of belonging. Onwards they flew until, eventually, the sight of the French coastline appeared ahead.

Looking down at the seventy-plus bombers, Victor could see them starting to make the bombing run when the whole sky around them erupted with anti-aircraft fire. It was nothing like he had ever experienced before as each aircraft began to jump and weave among the explosions. One bomber took a direct hit and was engulfed in a huge fireball, leaving barely a trace that it had ever existed. Victor stared in disbelief as seven young lives were taken in an instant and they were not even given a chance to get free and take to their parachutes. His own aircraft was rocked by another explosion and he had to 'catch' the Spitfire on its controls to regain normal flight. Down below he could see the warships moored in the harbour with British bombs raining down on them but he only took a fleeting glance as his current plight demanded all of his attention. He saw

another huge explosion and yet another bomber plunged earthward in a near vertical dive when suddenly the RT lit up with calls of 'Bandits!'. The whole formation was at the beginning of the slow and cumbersome turn for home when they were set upon by Bf 109s. Squadron Leader Boyd led his section into the attack and was able to dispatch two of the enemy machines before having to dive for cover. The intensity increased as 'B' Flight turned into an attack that came in from the port side but were grateful when the enemy machines buzzed overhead and away. They re-formed and continued to protect the formation from above, while swivelling their necks and keeping a constant look out for enemy attacks.

Flight Lieutenant 'Ginger' Lacey had been detailed to fly as 'top weaver', taking up the highest position in the formation, and had become involved in a dogfight with two Bf 109s. Climbing to 30,000ft, the trio twisted and turned, trying to gain the upper hand in this mortal duel. As 'Jim' was about to turn into an attack that was coming from his starboard side, he glanced up into his mirror and saw the chilling sight of the second aircraft looming large and pouring machine gun fire into his Spitfire. Bullets thudded into the armour plating behind his seat and he pulled away sharply to avoid the attack. He was outnumbered and flying for his life. Flying on the edge of blacking out, he threw the Spitfire around in an array of turns and climbs, trying to outfox his opponents but they worked well as a team and found their mark with attack after attack. Every time an opportunity came to fire, Lacey reacted in an instant but things were moving at a lightning pace and he couldn't deliver any kind of telling blow. Seconds turned into minutes and the three aircraft were locked in this dizzying dogfight. One of the enemy machines careered in from the port side and flashed in front of Lacey's Spitfire. In an instant he opened fire but was met with the sound of compressed air and the realisation that his ammunition had been expended. Added to this, he was burning fuel at an extraordinary rate but he had no choice but to fly his aircraft to its absolute limits in order to survive. 'Ginger'

Lacey had proven himself to be an incredible shot in the past but his survival now depended on his airmanship alone.

Time and again the German pilots worked together and attacked alternately from both sides and to the rear. Fear gripped 'Jim's' body as he threw his machine around trying to minimise the damage the attacks were causing. Another accurate burst found its mark and Lacey could feel his Spitfire showing the signs of damage as he sighted yet another attack coming in. In a last-ditch effort, he pulled hard back on his controls, with the Spitfire surging ever higher into the skies above Brest in an almost vertical climb. Seconds later he heard a huge explosion and, looking in his rear-view mirror, could make out the tangled mess of the two Bf 109s in a sheet of flames. They had collided in mid-air. One German pilot almost immediately baled out but the other must have been killed on impact as the enemy machines descended earthwards in a twisted, flaming mess. Looking around, Lacey could see no other aircraft around him and, exhausted, he set course for England. He would describe the combat as the scariest of his entire flying career.

The formation had fought its way back through the flak and out over the French coast but it had proven to be a very different raid from the Cherbourg attack. The defence of the two German warships had been quite staggering and, despite all of the efforts of the RAF, they remained moored in Brest harbour unscathed. Victor spent the entire homeward leg concerned about his fuel levels and was extremely grateful to sight the rugged coastline that signalled a return to RAF Predannack and an opportunity to refuel once again. Following this, the squadron flew back to RAF Chilbolton, landing at 1930. The defensive war of 1940 now seemed like a distant memory.

11

Living For the Moment

Despite the pressure and intensity of offensive missions, Victor was able to maintain an upbeat and positive demeanour. This was quite an achievement considering he had now been fighting on the front line for over a year and had experienced so much since joining 111 Squadron the previous summer. He had a very direct nature but was always somebody who treated others fairly and it was appreciated by those he served with. There seemed to be an almost permanent state of flux in the squadrons of Fighter Command, with personnel changing all the time. Whether it was due to promotion, postings or pilots being shot down, Victor was able to adapt to these changes and offer 501 Squadron some much-needed continuity. He was proving himself to be a natural leader, a consistently reliable member of 'B' Flight and a good man. Even under the dark clouds of war he was always thinking of others and this was typified when he sent his goddaughter, Marion, a toy panda bear for her third birthday on 29 July 1941. The following day he borrowed 'PT's' car and drove to Salisbury to meet Kim for some much-needed time with his love.

Once again 501 Squadron were about to experience another shake-up with a move to RAF Ibsley, to form part of the 'Ibsley Wing'. They would be tasked with providing escort cover for bombers that were detailed with attacking shipping at a place they were coming to know very well indeed: Cherbourg. It was proving to be incredibly dangerous work, which was hammered home to the squadron when Sergeant Beecham was shot down and killed over the Channel on

6 August 1941. Squadron Leader Boyd had also been promoted to wing leader and replaced by Battle of Britain veteran, Squadron Leader Christopher 'Bunny' Currant. 'Bunny', as he was known to all, was a modest man on the ground but a courageous and quite brilliant leader in the air. He had built a reputation of always putting his men first, of being incredibly enthusiastic and extremely efficient – it would prove to be another great appointment for the squadron. He had been brought to the officers' mess by Wing Commander Boyd who introduced him to 'one and all' before he almost immediately got to work with his new squadron. On 15 August, there was yet more change with the sad departure of one of the stalwarts of the squadron, Flight Lieutenant 'Ginger' Lacey. By now an absolute legend of

501 Squadron. Squadron Leader 'Bunny' Currant stands centre, with Bob Dafforn above, straddling the engine of the Spitfire. Victor is sitting in the middle position on the right wing with his good friend, Robin Wheldon, in front.

Fighter Command, 'Jim' had been one of the highest-scoring pilots to fight in the Battle of Britain and had been in the thick of the fighting for fifteen months. He and Victor had struck up a close association with regular trips away with Eileen and Kim but this enjoyable chapter was about to close as 'Ginger' was posted to spend some time as an instructor at 57 OTU. It was the start of a new era for the squadron.

Victor was impressed with the impact made by 'Bunny' Currant. On 17 August, after another raid to Cherbourg, the new CO gathered his men and started a discussion about the squadron's tactics. He had many new ideas of his own and willingly promoted open discourse about the best way the squadron could implement them. He had brought a new energy to the team and Victor was pleased when two days later 'Bunny' took him to one side to discuss the possibility of taking over 'A' Flight from 'Ginger' Lacey. It was a huge compliment to Victor and timely recognition for a man who had given so much. August 1941 saw relentless raids over Cherbourg covering RAF bombers but this didn't tell the whole story of life with the squadron. More often than not the evenings were spent attending parties, going to the pub with Daff, 'PT' and Wheldon or playing bridge in the mess. One cannot underestimate the bonds that this band of brothers would have formed during these intense times. Exposed, fighting over enemy territory, each pilot would depend on one another to 'do their job'. As their professional relationships developed, so did their personal friendships as, after a hard day's fighting, they would prepare for the inevitable night out. Whether it be to drink to a missing comrade, simply to relieve the stress and tension of the day's sortie or just to live as any twenty-something ought to, the boys from 501 Squadron became inseparable. These same evenings almost always included a call to Kim, with one diary entry simply stating the words 'Kim adorable.'

On 19 August 1941 Victor heard that he had officially been given command of 'A' Flight and put forward for promotion to flight lieutenant. Inwardly Victor was thrilled with his new role but he moved forward stoically, secure in the conviction that he'd never let his boys down. And so the pace continued, with the summer months becoming almost a blur as the squadron were detailed on relentless offensive operations. Images of burning bombers, of huge destruction as British bombs fell to the ground and intense dogfights for survival were ingrained into Victor's mind. His days were spent in a state of draining concentration and heightened awareness as he led 'A' Flight from the front, with the evenings becoming a much-needed release from these mental and physical demands. There was also an added sense of jeopardy to these operations as every pilot knew that if they were shot down, they faced the uncertain prospect of spending the rest of the war in a German prison camp. For Victor, the thought of being separated from Kim and life with the squadron was unbearable, so he moved forward with a strong and determined mindset, knowing that he'd do everything in his power never to let this happen. His love for Kim and their desire to build a future together was a huge motivator.

The move to RAF Ibsley also saw 501 Squadron chosen for a project that would represent a welcome change from operational flying and make them the subject of much attention as they became the film stars of Fighter Command. *The First of the Few* was a proposed film that would tell the story of the Supermarine Spitfire and its designer R.J. Mitchell. Starring David Niven and Leslie Howard, who would also go on to produce the movie, it sought to capture the feeling of the moment and celebrate Britain's achievements during the dark days of 1940, with the iconic story of the Spitfire taking centre stage. Fighter Command were more than happy to assist the project but there was a catch. Their squadrons were in the process of re-equipping with an updated mark of Spitfire, the Vb, which had cannon fitted to each wing, meaning they no longer looked like the Battle of Britain variants that carried Browning machine guns. No. 501 Squadron were still flying this earlier mark and, due to the fact that they were yet to receive their new aircraft, were chosen for the job.

RAF Ibsley was invaded by hordes of technicians and camera crews as the squadron filmed the battle and scramble sequences used in the movie. For the pilots of 501 Squadron, it proved to be a huge amount of fun and a welcome distraction from the rigours of offensive flying. Victor would lead the squadron during one day of filming and would also fly a captured Heinkel He 111 alongside Wing Commander Boyd that was being used for the battle sequences. Needless to say that after a hard day of filming, the squadron along with Niven and Howard would head out for the customary night's festivities, with Victor commenting: 'Niven was great company, we had some great fun.'

Above: David Niven, Co-star of *First of the Few*.

Opposite above: Stars of *First of the Few* David Niven and Leslie Howard.

Opposite below: David Niven and Victor looking relaxed during filming.

Above: Victor during the filming of *First of the Few*.

Opposite above: David Niven and Leslie Howard discuss filming with Victor and Anthony Palmer-Tomkinson.

Opposite below: David Niven, co-star of *First of the Few*.

September 1941 seemed to pass in the blink of an eye as the squadron continued with its offensive work over Europe, accommodated the film crews and were also re-equipped with their own new Spitfire Vbs. These were a vastly upgraded mark of aircraft that carried the powerful Hispano cannon and the squadron used the back end of the month to gain experience on type and test out this new armament. The difference between cannon fire and machine gun fire amazed the pilots from 501 Squadron. An accurate burst from the new armament could destroy an enemy aircraft in an instant and would prove to be a much-needed upgrade as the battle over Europe intensified.

Throughout September, the target continued to be Cherbourg as time and again the squadron would climb into uncertain skies and take the fight to Germany. It was also around this time that another dear friend, Flight Lieutenant 'Bob' Dafforn, left 501 Squadron for a well-earned rest from operations.

After a particularly tricky 'sweep' on 30 September, Victor was able to take a full week's leave from the squadron and once again be with Kim. The pair had been exchanging letters and were regularly speaking on the telephone, openly discussing the prospect of marriage. They clearly loved one another dearly but the demands of having a relationship amidst the uncertainty of war, alongside Victor's vastly diminished life expectancy, meant it was a subject that needed some consideration. Nevertheless, when the pair met in London on

1 October 1941, it was all they could talk about. They had dinner at the Cafe Royale and the following night went to the Trocadero, dancing into the night and living for the moment. On returning to their hotel, they spoke deep into the early hours and their decision was made. They loved one another and that was enough. The following morning the pair went shopping

Victor and Kim enjoy some time together whilst on leave.

at Selfridges and started to look for wedding rings. Kim saw her new fiancé off at King's Cross station as he made the journey back to St Neots to see his family, sharing the news of a November wedding with his mother and father.

On 9 October 1941 the squadron were once again filming for *The First of the Few* when they received an unexpected order to scramble and dashed to their waiting aircraft. It felt most heroic abandoning the demands of movie making to surge into the skies in squadron strength being watched by cast and crew alike. Once airborne, Squadron Leader Currant was vectored onto a plot that turned out to be an enemy Junkers Ju 88 reconnaissance aircraft flying at 18,000ft. Taking it in turns to fire, the entire squadron made an attack and shared in the destruction of the aircraft, seeing it go down in flames. They were airborne once again three days later with other squadrons on a raid over Cherbourg and Victor had the honour of leading 501 for the first time. It proved to be a relatively uneventful mission, with only moderate flak but 118 Squadron were more than happy with their haul of three Bf 109s destroyed. By now Victor had over 530 hours of flying experience under his belt and was one of the most experienced airmen on the squadron.

This demanding pace continued with regular convoy patrols, fighter sweeps and escort duties. On 13 October 501 Squadron took part in a tricky mission escorting Blenheims to Saint-Omer and were hounded by 'many 109s' during the trip, and then two days later were airborne once again escorting twelve Blenheims to Le Havre. This particular raid stuck in Victor's mind as, while the squadron were concentrating their efforts on yet more Bf 109s that were attacking the formation, his aircraft was hit by flak. It jumped and seemed to hang in the air for a second as if winded but the ever-reliable Rolls-Royce engine escaped damage and he was able to nurse the aircraft home with the rest of the squadron. On 24 October, and for the last major offensive action of the month, he once again led 501 Squadron. The destination was Cherbourg and despite not seeing any enemy

Members of 501 Squadron gather for a photo, 8 November 1941. Back Row Left to Right. Sgt Dvorak, Sgt Hargreaves, Sgt Campbell, P/O Stanbury, F/L Ekins, S/Ldr Currant, F/L Yule, P/O Greenaway, F/O Raba, Sgt Vendl, Sgt Cummings. Front Row L to R Sgt Lynch, Sgt Williams, P/O Drossaert, Sgt Vrtis and Sgt Rocovsky.

aircraft during the raid the flak barrage that was put up by the German defenders was some of the heaviest that he had ever seen. All of the pilots were grateful to get back to Ibsley that evening and enjoyed a wonderful dinner in the mess. The ensuing party would not end until 0100 hours but Victor still found time to write to Kim.

As 1941 progressed into the autumn, the weather conditions once again began to deteriorate, seriously restricting flying. The low cloud and fog did, however, support a new tactic being developed by Fighter Command, the controversial 'Rhubarb' operations. They were quite simple as small numbers of aircraft, usually pairs, would fly low into France and Belgium to shoot at targets of opportunity. They often made use of the protection given to them by bad weather conditions and the idea was to be on the offensive constantly. Targets such as staff cars, troop vehicles, lorries and trains were singled out and strafed with cannon fire but losses were common and questions were raised about whether losing pilots in this way could be justified. In 501 Squadron by far the biggest supporter of the 'Rhubarb' was Pilot Officer Anthony Palmer-Tomkinson. 'PT' had a relentless energy and was always keen to get at the enemy, and this new tactic offered him the chance to keep taking the fight to Germany. On 3 November he flew low over France and successfully destroyed three German lorries. The following morning, he was airborne once again with pilot officers, Newbury and Greenaway and Sergeant Dean, and the formation took it in turns to attack a German goods train. It all seemed so positive and that afternoon Pilot Officer Shore and Sergeant Lynch were keen to get involved so they headed out to France once again but this time were intercepted by Bf 109s. Pilot Officer Shore couldn't evade his attackers and was forced to crash land on a French beach with his Spitfire badly damaged. He would sit out the rest of the war as a PoW. Shortly after this, Pilot Officer Greenaway was lost in similar circumstances and was last seen going down trailing white smoke – he too would become a captive.

On 17 November 1941 Victor would have an emotional insight into some of the demands of leadership within a fighter squadron. The squadron had been ordered to take part in a large-scale 'Rhubarb' over France and Pilot Officer Stanbury and Sergeant Dean took off at 0940 hours, closely followed by Pilot Officer Palmer-Tomkinson and Sergeant Campbell ten minutes later. Weather conditions were horrific on both sides of the Channel but the two pairs individually got to work in looking for targets of opportunity to attack. Dean and Stanbury had attacked what they took to be a distillery, a transformer and some 'Hun' soldiers when Sergeant Dean was seen to 'fade away' into a rain cloud. Pilot Officer Stanbury started the search but could not find any trace of the pilot, who had lost control of his aircraft under mysterious circumstances. Sergeant Dean was reported as missing, presumed killed, and that evening his distraught mother visited RAF Ibsley to find out what information she could. Victor offered what words he could, knowing that nothing he could say would make up for her pain and suffering. He would simply write 'Dean missing. Saw his mother – distressing.'

It was during this pressure and intensity that Victor was able to take his leave from squadron duties for a short while and travel to Torquay to meet with family and friends before getting married to his beloved Kim. The squadron gave him a royal send-off on 22 November with a trip to Leonards pub with 'the boys'. The beer and banter flowed freely as all thought of battle was put aside for a 'merry evening' of celebration. He had asked Pilot Officer Robin Wheldon to be his best man and the two travelled up to Salisbury to meet Victor's mother and father before travelling together to Torquay. The next few days were spent blissfully in the company of friends and family as the pair received lots of presents and the champagne flowed. They were married on 25 November 1941 at St Mark's Church, Torquay. Kim was given away by her father and wore a powder blue suit, blue hat with a brown veil and brown accessories. She carried a spray of English orchids. They enjoyed a 'grand wedding', were humbled to receive thirty-five telegrams of congratulations and held the reception at the Imperial Hotel. Of the guests who attended, Victor was particularly pleased to see both 'Bob' Dafforn and 'Ginger' Lacey, despite their many service commitments. Later that day, Kim wore a brown coat and hat with matching accessories as she and her new husband departed the celebration and travelled to Norfolk Royale Hotel in Bournemouth to enjoy their honeymoon. It was while there that Kim received a pleasant surprise as a telegram arrived informing her that she was being promoted to acting section officer and would receive a full-time commission. The pair spent five wonderful days of shopping, resting and plenty of celebrating before they travelled to London to prepare Kim for her new position. She had been transferred to the Headquarters of Coastal Command at Northwood and would specialise in 'intelligence'. After shopping at Selfridges

Victor and Kim amongst the warmth of the Kimber family.

Victor and Kim were married on 25 November 1941. Back Row Left to Right. Sydney Ekins, Maude Ekins, Robin Wheldon, Joan (Kim's Cousin) and Cynthia Ekins. Front Row Left to Right. William Kimber, Elizabeth Kimber, Victor, Kim and May Kimber.

and Moss Bros. for her new uniform, the happy couple parted ways on 1 December 1941.

By now the winter weather had really set in and flying was extremely limited. On 6 December the squadron said farewell to Robin Wheldon, who had been posted overseas, and once again a merry evening was had at a dinner and dance party. Victor was, of course, sad to see him go but by now he was well versed with the comings and goings of friends and colleagues. No. 501 Squadron used this enforced downtime to play rugby, poker and bridge, and also to celebrate the year's achievements at a shared dance party with 234 Squadron. There was still time in 1941 for one last big push and that involved a 'grand assault on Brest' on 18 December. It would prove to be the largest assault on Brest yet undertaken, with three successive waves of bombers attacking the target. The defence put up

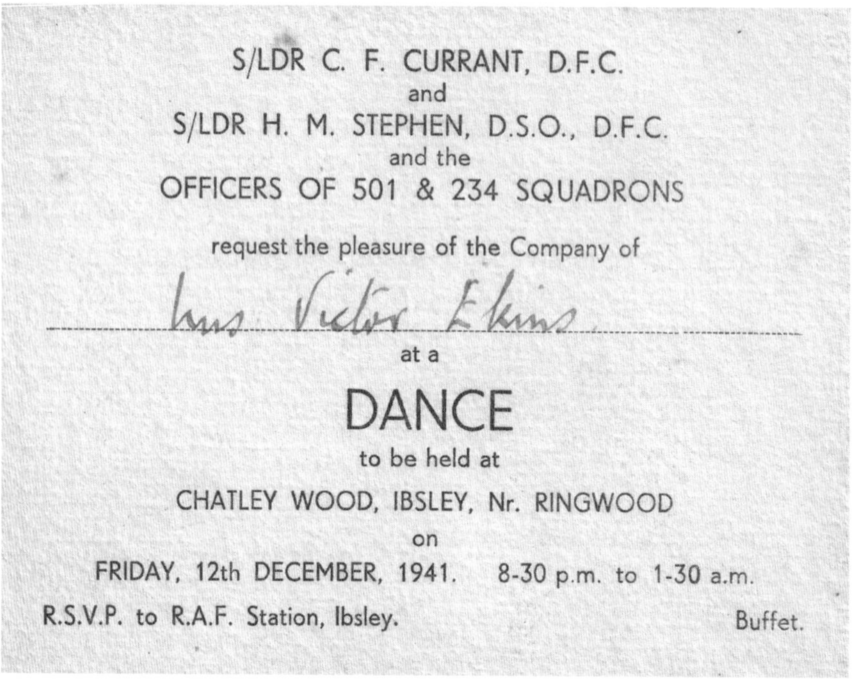

S/LDR C. F. CURRANT, D.F.C.

and

S/LDR H. M. STEPHEN, D.S.O., D.F.C.

and the

OFFICERS OF 501 & 234 SQUADRONS

request the pleasure of the Company of

Mrs Victor Ekins

at a

DANCE

to be held at

CHATLEY WOOD, IBSLEY, Nr. RINGWOOD

on

FRIDAY, 12th DECEMBER, 1941.   8-30 p.m. to 1-30 a.m.

R.S.V.P. to R.A.F. Station, Ibsley.   Buffet.

The invitation that was sent out for the 501 and 234 squadrons' dance, held on 12 December 1941.

by the anti-aircraft batteries was staggering, with the skies above the harbour described as being 'boiling with flak and smoke'. Victor was leading 'A' Flight, who were being harassed by four yellow-nosed Bf 109s, trying to tempt them into breaking formation and entering into a dogfight. One enemy aircraft persisted in making feint attacks trying to provoke a reaction, with another diving steeply through the formation. The squadron held their nerve and kept station protecting the bombers at 18,000ft. Victor was clearly able to see the carnage below and the bombs raining down on the harbour, and was incredibly grateful to land back at Ibsley at 1725 hours.

In rather bizarre circumstances the squadron then welcomed back Pilot Officer Robin Wheldon only a few weeks after his departure. He had been posted to the Middle East but the Wellington in which he was travelling had crashed into Gibraltar Harbour shortly after take-off. He was pulled from the wreckage and was one of only two people to survive the crash; a truly miraculous escape. He then returned to Milford Haven on a Royal Navy minelayer in the company of German prisoners and rejoined 501 Squadron on 21 December 1941. Later planned operations were cancelled due to bad weather and Victor celebrated the dawn of a new year in his hometown of St Neots at a dance party with his sister, Cynthia, that lasted until 0200 hours. It had been an intense year of operations that had seen him serving on the front line throughout. He was by now the only current member of 501 Squadron who had been with them during the Battle of Britain and an absolute rock to his men.

12

Goodbyes all Round

As with weather conditions the previous year, 1942 started out bleak and extremely cold. The squadron would have to battle weeks of snow, rain, fog, mist and gales that made consistent flying and regular offensive raids impossible. During the previous winter, the slower pace and unwinding of tension among pilots had been vital after the rigours and demands of the Battle of Britain. The squadron relished the change of atmosphere and Fighter Command used it to recharge, reorganise and replenish its squadrons. For Victor, the start of yet another year of war would have the opposite effect. For the previous six months he had been relentlessly on the offensive, dealing with the personal demands of offensive missions over occupied Europe as well as stepping into the role of leading and inspiring his men. The effort he had exerted was huge and he had very much adopted the mantra of the time to 'keep calm and carry on'. Ignoring a chronic lack of sleep and at times the unhealthy escapism found through evenings of drinking and late nights, he simply got on with the task in hand. Day in, day out he put personal thoughts and pressures to one side for the good of his flight and his squadron as a whole. He had been able to maintain this successfully due to the momentum and relentless nature of the work; he just did not stop. As a new year dawned and the weather conditions now forced him to stop, his body seemed to let go of all of the stress and tension that he had carried for so long, and he started to get ill. It wasn't an all-consuming illness that completely put him out of operational flying but more a continuous stream of colds, flu and headaches that made the challenge of leading his flight even harder. He was seriously run down and in need of a prolonged rest but duty called and that was enough for Victor to keep going.

One real tonic during this tough time was his friendship with Anthony Palmer-Tomkinson. 'PT' had a great capacity for making friends and was an incredibly popular member of the squadron but the friendship that he and Victor had forged was something different. Operationally, 'PT' was now Victor's deputy in 'A' Flight in much the same way as he himself had been for Bob Dafforn the previous year. Anthony would be tasked with blooding new pilots, of promoting the ways of the squadron and would be consistently by Victor's side on operations. He had a relentless energy and was by far the most active

Victor and Sergeant Campbell wait at dispersal wearing their 'Mae West' life jackets.

member of the squadron, getting airborne at any given opportunity. This however, was only half of the picture, as the two airmen began to form an almost brotherly bond. Victor was Anthony's 'best friend in the Royal Air Force' as the two shared nights out, games of squash, poker and even the much-maligned task of night-flying duties. From Victor's perspective, he looked out for 'PT' almost as if he were a big brother. His diary entries would, of course, include the comings and goings of his own day but he would also make note of those of his friend. Whether 'PT' was 'mending his car', out with the boys or in town 'courting', Victor logged it with the care and interest of a brother.

Despite his personal hardships, Victor had no choice but to keep pushing forward. On 10 January 1942, the squadron were hit with the news that Sergeant Eric Campbell had been lost whilst on a non-operational flight with Sergeant Thomas. The pair had taken off for air to sea practise firing over Bournemouth Bay when Sergeant Campbell's aircraft seemed to disintegrate in mid-air after pulling out of a shallow dive, killing him instantly. He had been with the

squadron for almost nine months and was an ever-present member of 'A' Flight. The sense of loss was enhanced when the late pilot's commission papers were received the same day that saw him promoted to pilot officer. Pilot Officer Eric

A rare picture of Victor with his good friend, Anthony Palmer-Tomkinson.

Campbell was laid to rest three days later with the whole of 'A' Flight in attendance. The poor weather would go on to dominate January 1942, along with Victor's ongoing illness as he ended the month with another 'shocking cold'.

He went to see the 'doc' on 3 February and was given leave away from operational flying to rest and recuperate but even this had no real impact as he returned still under the weather six days later. On 12 February 1942, the expected 'Channel dash' finally materialised where the German battleships the *Scharnhorst* and *Gneisenau*, the target of 501 Squadron for so long, made a break from their moorings at Brest Harbour for the safety of the German port of Wilhelmshaven. Victor knew these ships well and had seen them many times from the air among thick flak, and this was Germany's attempt at getting them both actively back into the war. They would have to run the risk of sailing directly up the Channel and had been waiting for favourable weather conditions to make their attempt. They set out in the early hours with a heavy escort of German destroyers and E-boats among low cloud and heavy fog.

An early morning 'Rhubarb' request by 'B' Flight, which would have almost certainly sighted the convoy, was rejected due to the weather conditions, and it wasn't until Group Captain Victor Beamish and Wing Leader Adrian Boyd sighted the convoy a few hours later that the alarm was eventually raised. In the absence of Squadron Leader Currant, Victor was put in charge of the squadron and they took off for RAF West Malling at 1305 hours to refuel and to get airborne with orders to maintain air superiority 15 miles off Ostend. Over the Channel the flying conditions were horrific, with the whole squadron battling the heavy rain and low cloud. Victor was frozen stiff, still suffering from illness and using every ounce of his strength to concentrate on finding the location of the convoy. After a long, exhausting and frustrating search they landed back at RAF West Malling at 1515 hours having not encountered any enemy aircraft or the convoy.

Below, the battle had raged. The collection of German ships had been protected by a strong force of Bf 109 and Fw 190 fighters and despite heroic efforts to attack the convoy by six outdated Fairey Swordfish torpedo bombers of the Fleet Air Arm, it remained on course. They had flown into withering crossfire on an almost certain suicide mission in an attempt to press home their attacks, with Lieutenant Commander Eugene Esmonde earning a posthumous Victoria Cross for his heroic efforts. RAF bombers then made an attempt to stop the formation but, by now it was too late and the German convoy made its escape. It was a huge opportunity lost for the Royal Air Force and the following months would be full of inquest and enquiry as to how it happened. As for Victor, he was exhausted and wouldn't get clearance from the 'doc' to get airborne again until 17 February 1942. It was a deeply frustrating time for a man who was usually so dynamic.

After a run of convoy patrols and shipping reconnaissance, the weather once again clamped down around RAF Ibsley and Victor was able to take a full week's leave. It was just what the doctor ordered and time with loved ones seemed to replenish his spirits and energy. It had been a tough start to the year, which was totally understandable seeing as though he had now been on the front line for twenty continuous months, but he was definitely starting to feel a 'little better'. He had the usual pang when leaving Kim, which was becoming stronger as their love deepened, but he was looking forward to getting back in the fold and easing his way back into life with a squadron on the offensive.

On arriving back at Ibsley he almost immediately received a call from Wing Commander Ian 'Widge' Gleed, who was commanding the Ibsley wing. The previous day, 501 Squadron had had quite a scrap and he wanted to fill Victor in with the latest 'gen'. The RAF had introduced a new tactic of trying to entice German fighters into combat by sending over large formations protecting a modest bombing force. On 9 March 1942, 160 Spitfires had been detailed to escort six Bostons on a raid to Mazingarbe. While over the target 501 Squadron had spotted twelve Bf 109s and pursued them down to 4,000ft, with

Squadron Leader Currant damaging one and Pilot Officer Newbury accounting for another. Out of nowhere, they were attacked by three Focke-Wulf Fw 190s that had been lying in wait and they poured fire into the squadron leader's Spitfire. He eventually managed to evade his attackers but had suffered serious head injuries, a graze on his forehead from a bullet strike and a damaged aircraft. Feeling faint from his injuries, he made for RAF Lympne but hadn't

Victor on leave at 28 New Street, St Neots.

realised that his tyres had been punctured during the attack and they dug in on landing, flipping the Spitfire over and trapping 'Bunny' Currant inside. With the cockpit rapidly filling with petrol fumes, the ground crews dragged him from the wreckage and took him to hospital, where he would spend a month recovering, leaving him with metal fragments lodged in his skull as a permanent reminder. The squadron now found themselves without a commanding officer and Wing Commander Gleed wanted Victor to fill the void. Once again, duty called and despite his own difficulties Victor stepped up and took command of 501 Squadron as offensive operations became more frequent.

For the next ten days Victor would lead the squadron from the front and the added responsibility seemed to have a galvanising effect, at

501 Squadron. The four pilots that are centre of shot are 'PT', Victor, 'Bunny' Currant and Robin Wheldon.

least in the short term. He had taken a deep breath, dug deep and made yet another Herculean effort. The second half of March would see multiple offensive missions to Cherbourg but also a return to the nights out with PT and the boys. Unfortunately, it would prove to be short-lived as the demands that were being exerted on him took their toll once again, and he fell ill with yet another 'nasty cold'. It was incredibly frustrating but a clear sign that Victor was in desperate need of a rest, and it hadn't gone unnoticed.

On 4 April 1942, 'PT' would prove beyond any doubt that he was the absolute master of the 'Rhubarb' mission as 501 Squadron were detailed with a job of some importance. The Luftwaffe had developed a tactic of using a radio beam as a navigational aid to attack their targets, which allowed them to bomb accurately at night, even in foul weather conditions. To counter this threat the squadron were ordered to attack a potential beam station site in the Cap de la Haque peninsula and Anthony, along with pilot officers, Newbury, Drossaert and Thomas, were chosen for the task. As they crossed the Channel, the weather conditions began to seriously deteriorate. Regardless, they flew on, glued to their aircraft's instruments as visibility outside was impossible. 'PT' led the attack but as they approached what he thought might be the target area, they were confronted by worsening conditions of mist and heavy rain, leaving the operation in jeopardy. At the last moment 'PT's' uncanny sixth sense spotted the masts in the murk below and he led the aircraft down to attack. Flying low and attacking with cannon, Anthony and his team took the German defences completely by surprise and managed to destroy the masts and return back to base practically unscathed. It proved to be a very successful mission indeed and the following day it was confirmed that the masts had been put out of action.

Victor was extremely grateful when Squadron Leader 'Bunny' Currant returned to 501 squadron on 7 April and announced that its members had been chosen to take part in a demonstration of tactical power at the British army base at Imber for Winston Churchill and other high-ranking chiefs of staff. The squadron were detailed to attack dummy troops on the ground after a squadron of Hurricanes had flown in low to attack such ground targets as dummy troops, tanks and vehicles. On 13 April 1942, Squadron Leader Currant led Victor along with Flight Lieutenant Yule, pilot officers, Newbury and Raba, and sergeants, Tomkins and Thomas, to Imber for a full-dress rehearsal of the event that was due to take place three days later. They would go on to bear witness to one of the most tragic and graphic friendly fire incidents of the entire war. Circling at only 1,500ft, they formed up, waiting for their turn to attack when a pilot of 175 Squadron came in low and opened fire on what he thought was a collection of dummy soldiers. He had been a last-minute replacement and had never flown over Imber before. Victor looked down, watching in horror as the pilot in fact opened fire on a large gathering of 'top brass' and dignitaries, killing twenty-five and injuring over seventy people. It was a sickening scene to witness and a tragic waste of life.

Change was coming for Victor and as much as he outwardly fought the prospect of life without 501 Squadron, inwardly he knew that it was time. Over recent months he'd been undertaking a lot of army co-operation work and an opportunity had opened up with 286 Squadron, who were looking for a new flight commander. With his experience it made him a perfect candidate for the job. No. 286 were a full-time army co-op squadron that operated a variety of different aircraft for local anti-aircraft batteries to practise range finding and firing but, importantly, they were non-operational. This meant an end to offensive missions over Europe and a chance for Victor to unwind and return to full fitness, both mentally and physically. On 22 April 1942 his posting was made official and the following day he took off, alone, in Spitfire W3840 for his final flight with 501 Squadron. In perfect flying conditions he threw the Spitfire around the skies above RAF Ibsley, knowing that it was the end of an era and wanting to soak up every last moment. Every last barrel roll, loop, turn and climb with a squadron that he had come to love.

Victor had experienced so much since those early days at RAF Croydon and the baptism of fire that he had been subjected to with 111 Squadron. He had contributed towards inflicting Germany's first defeat of the war during the Battle of Britain and had found out that he was able to cope personally with the intensity of combat. He had flown through 'The Hardest Day' and the first of the large-scale raids over London on 7 September 1940, and almost lost his life during combat with 501 Squadron on 27 September 1940. Coming back from this within weeks, Victor had then set about giving his all to his squadron and that attitude, along with his natural abilities, had seen him now command a position of leadership. For almost a year, he had contributed towards taking the fight to Germany with regular, nerve-jangling sweeps over Europe. He had also found love. Victor Ekins had given literally everything of himself over the past twenty-one months of front-line action and had become a rock to those around him. He was reliable, dependable, resilient, inspiring and genuinely cared for others. He was also a brilliant pilot.

As he danced among the clouds above Ibsley, his mind wandered to those he had served with and who had played a huge part in his own personal journey. Some faces were a blur, as time and the pace of events had dulled the memory into recollecting fleeting moments, but others were as prominent as ever. The voices, the laughter, the banter, the unforgettable feelings of pride and unity as they had surged time and again into uncertain skies. It had been such an intense period of his life and his body was heavy with emotion. Taking a deep breath, he entered the circuit above Ibsley and came in to land for the last time as a pilot of 501 Squadron. His ever present and loyal ground crew met his arrival, as they had done so many times before, and he thanked them all for their efforts. That evening he had dinner with 'Bunny' Currant, who would write in Victor's logbook: 'Very sorry to lose you. Good luck to a very fine Flight Commander.' That night, as expected, was spent with all the boys in the mess as they shared 'goodbyes all round'. It's unimaginable how prophetic these words would become.

The following day, 501 Squadron were detailed with providing top cover for a raid over a target they had come to know so well over the previous year, Cherbourg. Led by Flight Lieutenant Bob Yule, who had filled in for 'Bunny' Currant, they were viciously attacked by six Bf 109s, which made effective use of mist and cloud cover over the target to 'bounce' the squadron with frightening accuracy. Tragically, both pilot officers, Robin Wheldon and Anthony Palmer-Tomkinson, were almost immediately shot down and killed. Their aircraft were seen to plunge into the icy waters below with no sign of a parachute. Their loss was quickly followed by Sergeant Virtis, who also went into the sea, and Sergeant Rocovsky, who was seen to bale out but his parachute failed to deploy. Sergeant Ian Blair managed to somehow nurse his damaged aircraft back to England and crash land near the coast. In just a few minutes on that fateful afternoon, 501 Squadron had lost four of its best pilots. Of the eleven aircraft that had taken off, only six would return to Ibsley. One colleague said of Anthony: 'He was a gentle and kind man, there will never be another quite like Mr PT.'

Robin Wheldon and Anthony Palmer-Tomkinson had trained together at 55 OTU, were posted to 501 Squadron together in May 1941 and had tragically been killed within seconds of each other on 25 April 1942. Victor had lost his best man and his best friend. That evening, two of the heaviest words written in his diaries were simply 'Rang Kim.' One can only imagine the emotion of their conversation.

A few days later he took the time to write to both sets of parents. He would receive a response from Robin's mother on 14 June 1942:

Dear Mr Ekins

It was wonderfully kind of you to send the photographs and I am glad to have them.

I think of you and your letter about Robin so often. Food growing from dawn to dusk as I do, gives me plenty of time for thought, but little time to write letters, though I think you might soon have had one from me.

I think my husband suggested you coming to see us sometime if you, or you and Mrs Ekins have time and inclination. It would be a great pleasure to meet you both. We heard little of your wedding, Robin is uncommunicative as my husband might say here, partly the result of the rather witness box atmosphere in a legal home I expect!

I still wonder why the possibility of him being a prisoner is thought to be so remote. When no trace of either plane was found in the sea. Do you think there is no chance whatsoever that he and Antony Palmer-Tomkinson are prisoners, or came down over France, although they got back to within 6 miles of the English Coast?

You will have heard of Peter. He is to be married soon to a dear little girl of nineteen. I think they decided to tell us the news as a counter-blast.

With warmest thanks and hoping we may meet.

Yours very sincerely

Margaret L Wheldon

In a post-war letter from Anthony's father, James Palmer-Tomkinson, would write:

> In my heart I believe that Tony would have made good and got something worth having out of life. He had developed so well in his years in the RAF. He had views of his own, perhaps too much so, but a good fault; he was ready and able to take responsibility, e.g., his last raid on the wireless station on the Cherbourg peninsula and he had a great capacity for making friends. I think he would have grown into the sort of man the country needs.
>
> I have been thinking a lot about him lately. He would undoubtedly now be in Switzerland as one of the British Olympic Ski Team which his brother is captaining. It used to be a great joy to see the two skiing together. As quite a small boy you would see Tony flying down the steepest runs in his big brother's tracks. I know that Jimmy thought Tony was likely to become a better skier than he is himself, which is saying something. How Tony would have enjoyed a season racing against the best pros in the world. However, that is just a sideshow.

It truly was the end of an era and Victor moved to 286 Squadron with a heavy heart. It had been a devastating blow. He would go on to serve with them for less than a month, flying the Boulton Paul Defiant and Airspeed Oxford, but he was soon posted away from flying duties altogether with a transfer to 10 Group Headquarters on 20 May 1942. He needed time away to process all that had occurred in such a short period and to begin the process of mental, physical and emotional recovery before the next big push that was almost certain to come.

13

Squadron Leader

The environment in which Victor arrived at 10 Group HQ at RAF Box couldn't have been more different to that of a front-line fighter squadron. At 28 years old Victor had been seen as the 'old man' of 501 Squadron but now he was surrounded by seniority both in rank and age. The staff were either First World War veterans, now in advancing years with decades of experience with the RAF under their belt, or pre-war regulars who had climbed through the ranks. Victor would be working closely alongside generals, senior air staff officers and the commanding officer of 10 Group, Air Vice Marshal Augustus H. Orlebar. He had been a First World War pilot, had competed in the Schneider Trophy and had held the world air speed record. He had joined Fighter Command in October 1940 and had taken command of 10 Group in July 1941, being given the task of organising the defence of the south-west of England and south Wales. It was an intriguing transition for Victor as the boisterous atmosphere of daily life in a fighter squadron had been replaced with maturity, experience and a different kind of responsibility. Victor was once again the person in the room with the most to learn and he relished the challenge. He was also more than comfortable mixing with the upper echelons of the Royal Air Force. Long since his early days at the agricultural auction in St Neots, Victor was able to judge each person on their own merits and not get overawed by their social standing or status. Life at 10 Group HQ could never replicate the brotherhood of the squadron or excitement of flying a front-line fighter aircraft but it was different – and for the time being a change was as good as a rest.

On Thursday, 4 June, while attending a conference for the AOCs of the Royal Air Force, Victor found out that he had been awarded the Distinguished Flying Cross in recognition of his service with 501 Squadron. It was announced in *The London Gazette* on Tuesday, 23 June 1942, with the citation reading:

> This officer has carried out many offensive sweeps and reconnaissances, including attacks on shipping and ground targets in enemy territory, and has damaged 3 aircraft. He is a skilful and gallant Officer, whose indomitable spirit and cheerful courage have been an inspiration to his squadron.

The following day he was sent to RAF Croydon in a Miles Master and made his way into London to collect his DFC ribbon for his uniform. This milestone was celebrated with Kim over a lunch, where they enjoyed 'too many cocktails', and he also took the time to send telegrams home to tell his family of the news. While Victor had been with 286 Squadron he had barely socialised but at 10 Group, as he started to unwind, nights out once again became the norm. It was proving to be a very good tonic indeed.

A typical work day would see Victor organising exercises and arranging co-op work between the army and the air force. It would involve many meetings with 'top brass' and much paperwork. On 11 June he was invited back to RAF Ibsley for a party with 66 Squadron, which gave him the welcome opportunity to reconnect with some old friends and see the familiar faces of 501 Squadron. It was lovely to feel the atmosphere of the squadron once again and the celebrations went on long into the night, with Victor eventually getting to bed at 0400 hours. He rose the next day with a terrible hangover and flew back to Colerne, which was only a few miles from RAF Box, arriving

FOURTH SUPPLEMENT
TO
The London Gazette
Of FRIDAY, the 19th of JUNE, 1942
Published by Authority

Registered as a newspaper

TUESDAY, 23 JUNE, 1942

Air Ministry,
23rd June, 1942.

ROYAL AIR FORCE.

The KING has been graciously pleased to approve the following awards in recognition of gallantry displayed in flying operations against the enemy:—

Bar to the Distinguished Flying Cross.

Acting Squadron Leader George Kemp GILROY, D.F.C. (90481), Auxiliary Air Force, No. 609 Squadron.

Since this officer was awarded the Distinguished Flying Cross in July, 1940, he has destroyed an additional 7 enemy aircraft and damaged a further 2, making a total of 10 destroyed and 4 damaged. Under his command his squadron has met with considerable success in the destruction of enemy aircraft. He is a first class fighter pilot and an excellent leader.

Distinguished Flying Cross.

Acting Wing Commander Patrick Henry WOODRUFF (39806), Reserve of Air Force Officers, No. 404 (R.C.A.F.) Squadron.

On 17th May, 1942, this officer led a formation of bomber aircraft in the attack on the German cruiser "Prince Eugen." Despite interference from enemy fighters, Wing Commander Woodruff accomplished his task in a skilful and determined manner. Throughout, he showed great leadership and determination. He has commanded the squadron since May, 1941, and, by his personal example, has contributed largely to its high standard of operational efficiency.

Squadron Leader Camille Enright MALFROY (90019), Auxiliary Air Force, No. 66 Squadron.

This officer is a most efficient and courageous fighter pilot, whose example has contributed materially to the high morale and fighting spirit of the personnel with whom he has served. He has destroyed at least 4 enemy aircraft and damaged several others.

Acting Squadron Leader John Swire DINSDALE (40999), No. 42 Squadron.

On 17th May, 1942, this officer led a formation of Beaufort aircraft in an attack on the "Prince Eugen." Despite heavy fire from the cruiser and accompanying destroyers, a most determined attack was carried out. Squadron Leader Dinsdale has completed many operational sorties, including an attack on the Scharnhorst and Gneisenau in the English Channel. His leadership and skill are of a high order.

Acting Flight Lieutenant Victor Howard EKINS (63073), Royal Air Force Volunteer Reserve, No. 501 Squadron.

This officer has carried out many offensive sweeps and reconnaissances, including attacks on shipping and ground targets in enemy territory, and has damaged 3 enemy aircraft. He is a skilful and gallant officer, whose indomitable spirit and cheerful courage have been an inspiration to his squadron.

Acting Flight Lieutenant Richard Alfred NEWBERY (60104), Royal Air Force Volunteer Reserve, No. 118 Squadron.

This officer has participated in a large number of operational sorties over enemy territory. These sorties have included fighter sweeps, successful low level attacks against ground targets and ships at sea, and bomber escort flights. He has at all times shown the greatest keenness and enthusiasm for operational flying.

Acting Flight Lieutenant Dennis Arthur PARKINS (102961), Royal Air Force Volunteer Reserve, No. 15 Squadron.

One night in June, 1942, this officer was the captain of an aircraft which participated in a bombing attack on Essen. Despite unfavourable weather, industrial haze and smoke, and in the face of heavy anti-aircraft fire, Flight Lieutenant Parkins made repeated runs over his target to ensure accurate bombing. His aircraft was extensively damaged but, displaying fine airmanship, he flew it safely back to base. This officer showed great determination and devotion to duty

Victor's award of the Distinguished Flying Cross was announced in the London Gazette on 23 June 1942.

at 1000 hours. To battle the headache that he experienced all morning, while back at 10 Group he resorted to a tried and tested remedy: '4 aspirins and gin.' It seemed to do the trick.

On 15 June 1942, he then received some even more incredible news with a promotion to squadron leader, with effect from 20 May. It was timely recognition for a young man who had given his all and proved himself to be a natural and courageous leader. Within an eleven-day period Flight Lieutenant V.H. Ekins had become Squadron Leader V.H. Ekins DFC. With this significant promotion, he knew that at some point he was likely to get his own squadron but for now was happy to immerse himself in the daily routine at 10 Group and was intrigued by the change in perspective. His work allowed him to gain an insight into the overall strategic picture of the war and not just the daily events of the squadron. He would note with interest the 1,000-bomber raids that were being sent by night to bomb Europe as offensive operations increased. He also took great interest in the Fw 190 that had mistakenly landed intact at RAF Pembrey on 23 June, giving the Allies a chance to test the aircraft rigorously for weakness. This was vitally important and

Victor's DFC is announced in a local newspaper.

a massive coup as the Fw 190 had gained the upper hand in the aerial war over Europe, outclassing the Spitfire V.

There was also a very cathartic element to this period of Victor's life. He once again connected with playing the piano, which had always been a great joy to him having played from a young age. He was a talented pianist but in recent times this had manifested itself in beer-fuelled 'sing songs' with his squadron. Now though, he played alone, long into the night as his thoughts and emotions passed through his fingers and onto the keys. Particular songs that allowed him to lose himself were *Smoke gets in your eyes* and *As time goes by*. These solitary sessions gave Victor great comfort as he expressed himself through his music and found it to be a natural way to release emotion. The nostalgia that it evoked brought back happy memories of lost friends but also allowed him to celebrate his love for Kim. As the weeks turned into months, he began to unwind, recharge and reconnect with the humble force of nature that he had become.

The summer months of 1942 passed into autumn at a steady pace. Victor's workload was consistent and engaging, with each day being predictable compared with the uncertainty surrounding events with a squadron. Initially, he welcomed this change but as time went on he could feel a restlessness building up within. Opportunities to get airborne were extremely limited and he began to crave the life that he had once known so well. His work enabled him to keep a close eye on the squadrons in his group but it also had the effect of making him feel as if he was missing out. America's influence in the war had increased massively since the attack on Pearl Harbor on 7 December 1941 and Russia was giving everything as the battle with Germany raged at Stalingrad. The Eighth Army in North Africa seemed rejuvenated under the command of General Montgomery and they were holding their own against Rommel's Afrika Corps. More importantly for Victor, the battle in the skies above Europe was raging, and he wanted to play his part again. It was proving to be a pivotal time in the Second World War and the sense of duty within Victor could not be ignored.

On 17 November 1942 Victor was invited to Buckingham Palace to receive his DFC from King George VI. It was an incredibly special moment and he was proud to share the day with his family, who attended a lunch party at Piccadilly after the investiture. For some time, Victor had made his feelings known to his superiors

CENTRAL CHANCERY OF
THE ORDERS OF KNIGHTHOOD,
ST JAMES'S PALACE, S.W.1.

6th November, 1942.

CONFIDENTIAL.

Sir,

The King will hold an Investiture at Buckingham Palace on Tuesday, the 17th November, 1942, at which your attendance is requested.

It is requested that you should be at the Palace not later than 10.15 o'clock a.m.

DRESS Service Dress, Morning Dress or Civil Defence Uniform.

This letter should be produced on entering the Palace, as no further card of admission will be issued.

Two tickets for relations or friends to witness the Investiture may be obtained on application to this Office and you are requested to state your requirements on the form enclosed.

Please complete the enclosed form and return immediately to the Secretary, Central Chancery of the Orders of Knighthood, St. James's Palace, London, S.W.1.

I am, Sir,

Your obedient Servant,

Flight Lieutenant Victor H. Ekins,
D.F.C., R.A.F.

Secretary.

The Royal invite to the investiture held at Buckingham Palace on 17 November 1942.

about returning to an active squadron and two days later he was approached about the possibility of taking over a squadron of his own. He jumped at the chance. After six months away from 'the boys', Victor was ready to return to the fold and the opportunity presented to him was to take command of one of the most prestigious squadrons in Fighter Command. No. 19 Squadron, who were based at RAF Perranporth in Cornwall, had a history that stretched back to the First World War. They had been the first squadron to be equipped with the Spitfire in 1938 and had been at the heart of the Battle of Britain, as well as the offensive over Europe. Victor had often theorised about how he would run a squadron of his own, what tactics they would use and what atmosphere he would promote. He had learned so much from the many experienced commanders that he had served under but had strong ideas of his own and was sure that he could galvanise the squadron into a strong, cohesive and proactive fighting force.

The one big drawback to the proposal was Victor's lack of flying time over recent months and he almost immediately began to reacclimatise himself with flight. On 20 November 1942, whilst on a trip to RAF Colerne, he was able to do two trips in a Spitfire that lasted over two and a half hours. Within moments of getting airborne it felt as though he'd never been away and he joyfully threw the aircraft about the sky giving it everything that he had. He was blowing away the last of the cobwebs and it was rejuvenating. He and Kim then celebrated their first wedding anniversary in style with lunch at the Savoy before bidding farewell to his friends and colleagues at 10 Group with more 'goodbyes all round'. To prepare further for this new position, Victor pulled some strings and joined 66 Squadron for a short period of time as a supernumerary squadron leader. It was a squadron he'd known well while flying with the Ibsley Wing and it gave him the opportunity to go on offensive operations and reacclimatise himself with the feelings, emotions and dangers, without the demands of leading a squadron.

On 29 November, he lined up at the flight line of RAF Zeals for what would become a very memorable flight indeed. Flying a stripped-down Spitfire Vc, he was about to undertake a task that 66 Squadron had come to love: the altitude test. Without weapons or ammunition, it was an ongoing competition within the squadron to fly the Spitfire to the absolute ceiling of its performance, and it was about to be Victor's turn. Opening the throttle, he experienced

Squadron Leader Victor Ekins DFC.

that memorable surge of power as the Spitfire thrust forward, eager to get airborne and into the environment for which it was designed. Pulling back the stick slightly and opening the throttle further, he began to climb into a clear, crisp abendrot sky that was full of the late afternoon colours made by a sun getting low on the horizon. He aimed for a small cloud formation and took great satisfaction in bursting through the middle of it and out the other side. As he gained height, the sight of the south coast stretched out before him and he could clearly see France across the Channel. Onwards still and the beauty of the unfolding panorama struck him deeply. He had by now climbed to the top of the clouds, and beyond clear and beautiful skies waited for him. Upwards he went and with every thousand feet he gained, the scene that was unfolding became even more glorious. As the air began to get thinner and with the Spitfire's rate of climb now slowing down, a glance at the altimeter showed that he was flying at 39,000ft. It was the highest he'd ever flown and the closest to the heavens that he'd ever been.

He was overcome by a beautiful feeling of tranquillity and remoteness as he flew high over England. He was alone and it was humbling. There were no other aircraft in the sky, no immediate threat on the horizon and absolutely nothing above him except sheer autumnal beauty. Everything around him seemed still. He flew on, maintaining this remarkable height with a clear, empty mind and a full heart. A very real feeling of detachment fell over him and, for a moment, everything below him felt irrelevant. It was just him, his aircraft, this moment and an overwhelming feeling of not wanting to land. He took a deep breath and his shoulders noticeably dropped on the exhale. How incredible it was to be a pilot. To have the feeling of an aircraft responding to his every move. Not only that, but to be able to share this real privilege with his friends and colleagues who also would have experienced the depths of these moments. 'PT' knew this world. So did Robin. His mind turned to the brotherhood that he had experienced with his squadron and how much it meant to him. To be able to share these moments and this huge turning point in history with like-minded people was so very important to him and something that he had missed dearly. With one last deep breath and a final scan of the horizon, savouring its beauty, Victor half-rolled the Spitfire and started to dive.

In stark contrast to the previous blissful minutes, the noise within the Spitfire picked up as Victor plunged earthwards, holding firmly onto the control column as the forces exerted on him increased. He felt alive. Now plummeting down to earth, he noted with some interest the unwinding on the dials on the instrument panel as his altitude decreased. His body braced under the G-force, as it had done so many times before, and he determinedly headed back to civilisation. Back to a reality that would soon see him lead a squadron of his own and a sense of pride flushed through his body. His own squadron. He was more determined than ever to lead his men from the front, to share their experiences and to serve them as best he could. Duty had called and he was once again ready for the fight. It was a great feeling to touch down once again at RAF Zeals and report the altitude of his flight. It had been the highest yet recorded but that only told half the story.

After an uneventful offensive sweep on 6 December escorting fifteen Liberators to Abbeville, Victor thanked 66 Squadron for their assistance and packed his belongings before making the journey to Perranporth the following day. He was met at the station by Flight Lieutenant Cox, who took him back to base and before long his pilots gathered in the mess. There was plenty that Victor needed to know about his new squadron and the men were more than happy to fill him in with the latest 'gen' about their experiences fighting the Luftwaffe. The gathered crowd then moved to the Stork Club and Victor eventually got into bed just before midnight, after an exhausting day. It was the beginning of an exciting new chapter in his life.

14

Nineteen

Victor had always been a person with a real fire inside him and, as he settled into life as a squadron leader at RAF Perranporth, it began to burn brightly once again. Perranporth was a beautiful place to be stationed with its sandy beach and rugged coastline but flying conditions could be tough during the winter months with its exposed position being battered by Atlantic wind and storms. This was his second tour of active duty and his new pilots very much respected that fact. They were the next batch to come through training with Fighter Command and had only ever known offensive operations. To them, like the rest of the nation, the pilots who had fought through the Battle of Britain were held in very high regard. In fact, they were the reason that many had joined the RAF in the first place. Victor had a natural presence about him, he'd experienced so much throughout his time as a front-line fighter pilot and had 'seen it all before'. His new squadron was a multicultural collection of airmen from Australia, New Zealand, Greece, Argentina, Rhodesia and Britain, who almost immediately trusted their new commander and, in time, would follow him anywhere.

The bad weather hampered flying opportunities throughout December 1942 as the squadron battled through the gales to fly 'instep patrols' 40 miles west of Brest. These were a new operation introduced to restrict the losses felt by Coastal Command aircraft on anti-shipping missions by maintaining an aerial presence on the west coast of France and around the Bay of Biscay. After a few local

Victor at 'B' Flight dispersal, RAF Perranporth. Photo Credit Roger Llywelyn Henderson.

flights to acclimatise himself with the surrounding area, Victor led 'A' Flight on 11 December as he began to get to know his new squadron both on the ground and in the air. He would lead them on a similar mission once again just three days later, experiencing a very tricky landing back at Perranporth in strong wind and gales where he 'nearly pranged' his Spitfire.

Victor's natural leadership qualities were evident from the start of his time with 19 Squadron as he displayed a real understanding of people and how to get the best out of them. The personnel under his command soon realised that he wasn't at all interested in himself but was far more interested in helping those around him. If they had a problem then Victor would actively listen and guide them towards finding a solution. If he thought somebody had potential then he did his utmost to draw it out of them by empowering them to do more. He was immediately recognised as a cheerful and fair leader but there was a line within him that should not be crossed. It soon became abundantly clear that pushing the boundaries and crossing that line was not a very good idea at all, as one airman found to his cost on 19 December with 'seven days confined to camp'.

As flying time was limited due to the weather conditions, Victor took the opportunity to start putting his stamp on the squadron. An early change at RAF Perranporth saw the introduction of sun lamps, which was quite a forward-thinking move having experienced the therapeutic use of ultraviolet lamps during his time with 501. It was a clear sign that Victor was acutely aware of the need to manage his pilot's well-being in order for them to function over a prolonged period of time as a front-line fighter pilot. The use of the sun lamps did have some drawbacks however, as on one occasion with 501 Squadron he noted 'Doc gave us 7 mins back and front sun ray – Set Bill's chest on fire and had some difficulty putting it out.' It was also during this period of bad weather that a regular routine of physical exercise was introduced to the members of 19 Squadron. December 1942 would see them play regular games of rugby, hockey, football and undertake physical training sessions on the beach at Perranporth. The sense of togetherness was promoted by challenging 130 Squadron to matches that often ended up in the mess, as the drinks flowed into the early hours.

On 23 December 1942, Victor led 'B' Flight on a two-hour instep patrol in the morning before leading the squadron on a sweep over Morlaix in the afternoon. After a quick wash and freshen up he then accompanied his men to the Stork Club and contentedly watched on as they partied and sang into the night.

Within a matter of weeks of arriving at his new squadron, Victor could sense the high mood and strong bonds that were forming. There seemed to be a strength in depth among the ranks and even the lesser experienced members came across as being willing to listen and learn. As 1942 drew to a close, a very satisfied Victor met up with Kim and the pair enjoyed seven days leave together away from the demands of service life.

The new year started with a flurry of convoy patrols as Victor became accustomed to life with his new squadron. He had inherited two very capable flight commanders in Flight Lieutenant 'Dingers' Bell and Flight Lieutenant Cox. Both were experienced airmen, with 'Dingers' particularly

A ST. NEOTS HERO.—Squadron Leader Victor Howard Ekins, D.F.C., the 29-year-old son of Mr. S. V. Ekins, St. Neots, who to-day commands the first squadron to be equipped with Spitfires. Joining the R.A.F.V.R. in 1938, Sq./Ldr. Ekins was commissioned in 1941 and is married to a Section Officer in the W.A.A.F. During the Battle of Britain he fought in some of the fiercest engagements and one day in September, 1940, had one of the most remarkable escapes on record, when a bullet went right through him and wrecked the controls in the cockpit. After baling out, he landed — by a curious chance — among an ambulance unit!

A newspaper cutting of a 'St. Neots Hero'.

being noticed by Victor as a fine leader. On 7 January 1943 the squadron then welcomed two new Australian sergeant pilots, John Baragwanath and Frank Cooper, who he described as being 'good types'. One person who became a particularly close ally to Victor was 19 Squadron's intelligence officer, 'Spy' Dilkes. Short in stature but with a huge personality, 'Spy' was full of experience and as tough as they came. He had been incredibly helpful with regard to giving his new commanding officer the 'gen' and this close professional relationship had led to the pair enjoying many nights out together. Flying Officer 'Jonnie' Foster also made an immediate impression, as did the rock-solid sergeant pilots, Tommy Rippon and Alan Glover. Everybody seemed to be in high spirits and ready to go on offensive operations.

On 15 January the squadron formed up at RAF Perranporth, with Victor leading from the front, and took off to rendezvous with twelve

Left to Right: 'Spy' Dilkes, Frank Cooper, Ian Mundy and Bill Mills.

Bostons that were detailed to bomb Cherbourg docks. In clear skies and beautiful sunshine, the squadron joined up with 234 and 130 squadrons and climbed to 19,000ft, enjoying unlimited visibility. The French coast was crossed west of Cherbourg and then a wide sweep was made before Victor was gratified to witness accurate bombing over the target area. Despite warnings of enemy fighters and incredibly heavy and accurate flak, the squadron landed back at base without incident at 1250 hours. It had been a very successful first offensive operation in squadron strength and Victor found out later the same evening that he had been appointed deputy wing commander flying, which led him to an immediate self-imposed 'vice ban'. This added responsibility could potentially see him lead three squadrons operationally and he decided that a clear head would be in order.

Three days later 19 Squadron took part in a 'Roadstead' operation, escorting three Westland Whirlwinds alongside 130 Squadron. These were small-scale operations generally flown at zero feet designed to seek out and attack German shipping along the coast of occupied France. Victor led 'A' Flight, which consisted of six aircraft in total, as the formation headed determinedly out to sea, only a few feet above the waves. After forty minutes they sighted the small island of Ushant, just off the coast of Brest, when 'Dingers' voice could be heard over the RT warning of 'bandits'. Four Fw 190s had been sighted, also flying at sea level in a north-westerly direction but out of range to be an immediate threat. Weighing up the situation, Victor was about to give orders to break formation and attack when a further two Fw 190s were spotted to their left about to open fire. It had been an ambush tactic employed by the enemy force that they had executed almost perfectly. The whole formation broke and a dogfight erupted where Flight Lieutenant Bell and Pilot Officer Conner were able to damage the two enemy machines. Sergeant Glover had been caught in the melee and received many hits to his aircraft but was able to land back at base successfully despite being seriously injured due to a cannon shell that exploded under his seat. Bleeding profusely, he had turned his oxygen supply on to full and somehow navigated back to RAF Perranporth, executing a perfect landing. As other members of the squadron rushed to the badly damaged Spitfire it soon became clear how seriously injured Glover was and he was lifted out of the cockpit by the huge frame of Sergeant Baragwanath and rushed to Truro Hospital. Sadly, Sergeant Sloan had also been caught in the attack and was seen to go down into the sea. This led Victor to write the first of the many letters home to next of kin that he'd be forced to write over the coming months, such were the demands of life as a squadron leader.

The engagement had really highlighted to Victor how outclassed the Spitfire V was compared with the quicker and better-armed Fw 190s. The long-awaited arrival of the upgraded Spitfire IX had begun throughout certain squadrons of Fighter Command but, for now, 19 Squadron would have to wait their turn. He paid Alan Glover a visit the following afternoon and was pleased to see him in good spirits. The squadron would go on to visit him on many occasions throughout his recovery, generally as a precursor to a night out in Truro. Over the next ten days, Victor would lead the squadron from the front on a further four occasions as they flew bomber escort missions and offensive sweeps. He was leading by example and becoming accustomed to the life of the squadron leader. It was a life of combat, responsibility, man management, conflict resolution, planning and paperwork, and very soon he would also have to add logistics to this ever-expanding list.

On 9 February 1943, 19 Squadron were released from operational flying duties to take part in a large-scale training exercise named 'Spartan'. It was led by General Bernard Paget with an emphasis on co-operation between the Army and Air Force in preparation for an Allied invasion of occupied Europe. Victor had been suffering from a bad back since the beginning of the month but regular treatment at Truro Hospital had eased his pain and he set about preparing for the challenge. No. 19 Squadron would attend many briefings and lectures about the up-and-coming exercise and Victor would be continually occupied with the logistical challenge of leading a squadron on the move. This meant making provisions for the entire unit and support personnel including equipment, kit, supplies, food and the tents that they would be expected to sleep in. The idea behind 'Spartan' was to learn as many lessons as possible about the demands of operating a fighting force that is constantly on the advance. For Victor, this prompted many meetings with a variety of personnel from 19 Squadron as they prepared and catered for the unknown. For the remainder of February, the squadron were fully focused on 'Spartan' and that included yet more physical exercise, including runs, football and PT sessions on the beach. On 20 February Kim was able to take a week's leave and Victor proudly introduced her to his 'boys'. The pair would enjoy memorable evenings in the mess as well as long and 'grand' walks on the beach. On 27 February 1943, 19 Squadron left RAF Perranporth after receiving a movement signal instructing them to fly to RAF Middle Wallop. Spartan was about to begin.

On 1 March 1943 the squadron arrived in force and set about preparing for 'offensive' operations. The exercise was essentially a staged invasion of Great Britain with two designated fighting forces, both offensive and defensive, involving both the army and Air Force. It was going to be a large-scale manoeuvre, judged by umpires, that could prove vitally important to the success of the real Allied invasion of Europe. To really highlight how self-reliant 19 Squadron were expected to be, ten of the squadron aircraft flew carrying 90-litre drop tanks filled with fuel. Another six aircraft carried the same-size tanks but were instead carrying vital equipment. On landing at Middle Wallop, all pilots then refuelled by themselves from the fuel they had carried and were ready for the operation within an hour and fifty minutes. The next two weeks were spent living under canvas, in cold conditions and carrying out defensive patrols whenever possible. No. 19 Squadron successfully escorted Hurribombers on 'attacks' at Swindon, Buxford and Chipping Norton, and also enjoyed their most successful day of

Flying Officer Bill Mills.

The basic living conditions of 19 Squadron's campsite during Operation Spartan.

Flying Officer Dennis 'Handley' Page wearing a tin hat alongside an unknown pilot of 19 Squadron.

operations while attacking Newmarket and Bottisham aerodromes. With Victor leading the squadron, the umpires adjudicated that nine 'enemy' machines had been damaged with a further nine 'destroyed' with no losses. It was the most enjoyable sortie flown during Spartan.

The exercise proved to be a great success with many vital lessons learned. For Victor, the biggest challenge by far was looking after his squadron and keeping them in a fit state to fight. Food was scarce, living conditions were poor, the weather was freezing cold and the tents leaked. Scrounging food was a constant challenge for the squadron, with both Victor and Sergeant Baragwanath proving the most adept, acquiring 'butter and jam' and dishing out 'eggs, oranges, milk and chocolates'. From an operational standpoint, the high standards with which Victor operated were apparent from the start and he highlighted an issue that needed immediate attention by Fighter Command. He was shocked at the lack of discipline shown by other squadrons while using the RT, commenting 'RT natter by 182 shocking and their attack not much good.' He had experienced first-hand the need for discipline on the radio during battle and his anger would prompt him to 'have a row' with his opposing squadron leader before reporting the matter up the chain of command.

The time spent under the canvas did have an extremely galvanising effect on the squadron, however. They shared the discomforts as one and would spend the evenings sitting around the campfire together. 'Dingers' let this tent become the squadron casino as card games, in particular poker were a regular occurrence. On 11 March the boys enjoyed a few beers, with 'Spy' Dilkes having three pints and getting 'pickled', and then the following night they shared a few more and sang around the campfire. Sergeant Baragwanath would reflect after the war: 'I shall miss the many friendships I have made, especially those which began under the dreaded canvas.' On 12 March 1943 'Spartan' officially ended and all officers and NCOs were incredibly grateful to visit the mess at RAF Middle Wallop, with the squadron ORB commenting 'Words cannot describe our feelings to a real meal and the change to the usual bully beef and biscuits.'

19 Squadron pilots sit around the campfire during Operation Spartan.

With 'Spartan' now behind them, the squadron were keen to get back to operational flying but were about to experience a period of frustration and change that Victor was forced to manage carefully. They remained at RAF Middle Wallop until the end of the month before moving to RAF Fairlop on 5 April 1943 – once again living under the dreaded canvas. After a period of bad weather that seriously restricted flying, Victor dusted off the cobwebs by leading the squadron on an evening formation flight to a destination that he knew well – St Neots. In perfect formation, twelve Spitfires roared over his home town, much to the delight of his family and friends, who watched on with pride. They were then detailed with yet another training exercise named 'Welsh', which saw them collaborating with the Canadian Army. It proved to be another very useful opportunity for learning but was made all the more difficult as the squadron endured camping in horrific weather conditions with leaking tents that regularly blew down. Their next operational offensive sortie would not take place until the middle of May.

By now the squadron were absolutely desperate to get back down to business and once again take the fight back to Germany. On 15 May they got their opportunity and were detailed as close support to twelve Bostons attacking Poix aerodrome. While over the target area they were attacked by twenty enemy fighters and a huge scrap developed in the skies above France. No. 19 Squadron's new Flight Commander, Flight Lieutenant Wigley, who had replaced Flight Lieutenant Cox, was able to press home his attack and damage a Bf 109. The enemy response was persistent and fierce, and Pilot Officer Eric Opie was seen going down, omitting white smoke during the engagement. The bombers were escorted home without loss and the squadron landed back at RAF Fairlop at 1750 hours. That evening 'the boys' went to Chigwell for a hard-earned night out.

The following day they were once again on the offensive, escorting six Mitchells attacking Caen aerodrome. They faced heavy flak during the flight but no enemy aircraft were seen and landed

Flight Lieutenant Philip Wigley.

back at Fairlop without incident. Just as things seemed to be settling down for the squadron, they then received the unwanted news that they were about to be posted back to RAF Perranporth. Everybody was extremely disappointed at the thought of moving back to a quiet corner of the country when all the squadron wanted to do was stay where all the action was and take the fight to Germany. Victor spoke to his squadron and immediately gauged their reaction, commenting that the 'boys were brassed off'. In his opinion, after spending the last few months moving from base to base and contributing towards training exercises, 19 Squadron deserved their chance to stay in the fight. The very same day that they had received the order to move, Victor had lunch with the Air Officer Commanding, where he was at his persuasive best and the decision was immediately overturned. The squadron would still be on the move but this time to RAF Digby in Lincolnshire, where they would be working closely supporting Bomber Command. The whole squadron were thrilled at the change of heart and enjoyed a night out in London before their move north. Victor took the opportunity to meet Kim and the group partied until 2330 hours, despite three air raids over the capital.

Once again Victor had to manage and negotiate the logistics of uprooting and moving his entire squadron and support personnel but within days they were comfortably accommodated at RAF Digby, and ready to carry on the fight. On 22 May 1943 the squadron took part in making 'dummy' attacks on a Lancaster that was being flown by a squadron operating from the same base and Victor took the opportunity to fly inside the bomber to assess the effectiveness of the attacks for himself. Two days later they escorted thirty-two Beaufighters that successfully attacked a German convoy before Victor then had the opportunity to fly to RAF Wellingore and test the new American fighter, the Mustang. It had been an extremely busy few days and it was about to get busier. That evening RAF Digby welcomed the flight of what Victor described as 'the Hun circus'. This was actually the 1426 EAC Flight, who flew and maintained the captured German aircraft that were so vital for testing and gaining the upper hand during combat. Affectionately known as the 'Rafwaffe', they had arrived at the base in advance of a very special visit that was due to take place the following day. On 27 May 1943 King George VI and Queen Elizabeth visited RAF Digby, which proved to be extremely memorable for the squadron. During the morning, the royals had spent time with 617 Squadron at RAF Scampton, in the company of Guy Gibson, the commanding officer of the 'Dambusters'. Their historic raid had taken place ten days previously and King George VI had taken the time to congratulate each member of the aircrews who had been involved. Later that same day, they made the short journey to RAF Digby, where Victor was incredibly proud to introduce the royal visitors to his squadron. Lined up and looking immaculate, the pilots took it in turn to be presented to the king and queen, who spent quite some time chatting to the Australian members of 19 Squadron before enjoying a cup of tea in the mess.

The King and Queen inspect a captured Heinkel He- 111, now flying with 1425 EAC Flight, known to Victor as 'the Hun Circus'.

Victor proudly presents 19 Squadron to their majesties the King and Queen at RAF Digby, 27 May 1943.

Spirits were high within the squadron and, despite some more poor weather, the pilots were becoming an exceedingly tight group indeed. The month of May was rounded off with a party at a local pub that didn't end until 0200 hours. Each member took their turn in writing their name on the ceiling before 'Spy' Dilkes was seen to be wandering around 'minus his clothes'. What was also becoming apparent during this period were those members who Victor trusted as his inner circle. These were the men who had proven by their actions that they could be relied upon and trusted by their squadron leader. Sergeants, Baragwanath and Cooper, were always there to support Victor, as was the irrepressible 'Spy' Dilkes. One person who had really proven himself over previous months was Flight Lieutenant 'Dingers' Bell. As Victor's responsibilities had increased, he had found that Bell had been a natural leader who was more than capable of stepping up and leading the squadron in his absence. A popular member of 19 Squadron, 'Dingers' had accompanied Victor on many nights out as the two became firm friends.

On 2 June Victor and 'Dingers' travelled to RAF Matlaske to negotiate and plan yet another move for the squadron. They would now be based in Norfolk, with a promise of more offensive operations to look forward to. This constant upheaval was due to the creation of the Second Tactical Air Force, which had been conceived specifically for aerial support of the proposed invasion of Europe. It involved an entirely new structure, chain of command and co-operation between fighters and bombers, with 19 Squadron finding itself at the heart of the change. The process of managing and implementing this huge shift in dynamic was extremely complicated, as new wing commanders were appointed, briefed and then set about the task of readying their squadrons for tactical operations. The Allied powers were serious about taking the fight back to Hitler and this was a clear indication that the invasion of occupied Europe was at the forefront of their mind. Despite the upheaval, Victor was thrilled that 19 Squadron had been assigned to 122 Wing, which was led by his former commanding officer at 501 Squadron, Wing Commander Christopher 'Bunny' Currant. He in turn would be supported by another Battle of Britain veteran, Wing Commander Flying Harold Bird-Wilson, who would lead the wing in the air. 'Birdie' as he was known to all, was a popular figure and an inspirational leader. He had ten aerial victories to his name and was regarded as an aggressive and dynamic fighter pilot who never backed away from a fight. No. 122 Wing would be made up of three experienced squadrons, with 19 being joined by 122 and 65. Another added bonus to this restructure was the reconnection with Squadron Leader James Ritchie, who commanded 132 Squadron at the neighbouring 125 Wing. Ritchie had been a fellow sergeant pilot with Victor during the early 111 Squadron days. He had flown by Victor's side on 5 September 1940 as one of only four Hurricanes to attack a fighting force of 120 enemy aircraft, and had experienced

Sitting centre of shot, then Squadron Leader, is Wing Commander Flying Harold Bird-Wilson, who led 122 Wing.

a similar rise through the ranks of the RAF. Victor found himself at the heart of a very experienced team that was full of friends and colleagues who he knew well and trusted explicitly.

The squadron once again packed up and on 4 May 1943, eighteen Spitfires flew to the new base at RAF Matlaske, with 'Spy' Dilkes put in charge of organising the remainder of the squadron who arrived by road at 1900 hours. Here they flew escort missions and a flurry of shipping reconnaissance but, within two weeks, the inevitable happened and they were ordered to move once again. Victor was getting airborne as much as he could but was finding that his time was being occupied with meetings and logistics. The squadron were desperate to settle at a base of their own but for now would have to endure the frustration of upheaval as the Second Tactical Air Force found its feet. On 20 June 1943 they arrived at RAF Gravesend. On 2 July, they were moved once again, this time to RAF Newchurch.

'Spy' Dilkes, in uniform right of centre, oversees yet another squadron move.

Newchurch was one of a number of advanced landing grounds that had been built in Kent, with accommodation and amenities being very basic indeed. The squadron would be living under canvas and would endure weeks of poor and insufficient food. Victor invested in a new camp bed in an attempt to improve his sleeping conditions but it made little difference as he, and the rest of the squadron, struggled. Somehow, despite constant change and many challenges, spirits remained high within the squadron, as did the willingness and desire to get into battle. They were still as motivated as ever to go on the offensive and take the fight to Germany.

Victor enduring life under 'the dreaded canvas'.

15

The 100th Hun

The move to RAF Newchurch triggered a very intentional push to keep the squadron's standards high and to be prepared for the moment when they were called into action. Every single member of 19 Squadron worked tirelessly, in blistering heat to set up their new camp, organise equipment and begin the process of camouflaging their aircraft. Conditions were so hot that Victor got badly sunburnt on his back and one of the sergeants' tents managed to catch on fire. For three days they toiled, with Victor putting in extra shifts behind the scenes acquiring extra supplies and food so his squadron would be as comfortable and as energised as possible to play their part in 122 Wing. Conditions were far from ideal but they had long since learnt how to put up with the hardship of constant change and living under canvas. On 5 July 1943, Victor led the squadron on a cross-country flight to acclimatise them with their new surroundings. They had all put in a massive effort over the preceding days and Victor was immensely pleased with the results and the attitude of his men. He now considered 19 Squadron to be on the 'top line' and ready for action. Each morning they rose at dawn preparing themselves for combat only to be left disappointed as potential offensive operations were either cancelled at the last minute or allocated to other squadrons but on 9 July that would all change.

The squadron were detailed with flying close escort to twelve Mitchells that were to attack the marshalling yards at Saint-Omer. Taking off at 0715 hours, Victor led the squadron as they rendezvoused with the bombers before climbing to 11,000ft. It was a great feeling to be airborne once again after so much disruption, with the twelve Spitfires looking resplendent in fine weather conditions. Visibility was superb and the squadron could clearly see the bombs falling earthwards, although they were forced to report inaccurate bombing of the target area by the Mitchells. The formation recrossed the French coast at Gravelines and, despite encountering light flak, were able to escort the bombers back across the Channel. The high mood and enthusiasm that the squadron were experiencing was about to be tragically marred by an incident that would stay with Victor for the rest of his life. As the squadron approached RAF Newchurch and entered the circuit to execute a 'break away' landing, which required perfect timing, Flight Lieutenant 'Dingers' Bell and Squadron Leader Ekins collided, rendering both aircraft uncontrollable. They were a mere 1,500ft above the ground and each man only had seconds to react. In an instant, Victor pulled back the canopy of his Spitfire and successfully baled out, touching down on the airbase only moments after he'd taken to his parachute. He had cut his hands in several places and suffered severe bruising to his legs due to the impact but had escaped largely unscathed. Flight Lieutenant Bell had not been so fortunate. He had also managed to free himself from his stricken aircraft but his parachute had opened too late to save him. It was a huge tragedy and a massive loss for 19 Squadron.

'Spy' Dilkes had witnessed the collision from the ground and rushed across the airfield towards Victor. As he approached, he found his CO to be in a state of shock and absolutely mortified at what had occurred. Victor was devastated and 'Spy', being the experienced serviceman that he was, knew that he had to take action. He had seen many airmen over the years lose their nerve after such incidents, never being able to regain fully the confidence and attitude needed to pilot an aircraft again. He grabbed Victor by the shoulders and began to physically shake him back to reality. As much as he knew it was the last thing his CO would want to do after such an event, 'Spy' implored

Flight Lieutenant Patrick 'Dingers' Bell. Photo Credit Peter Wass Collection.

Victor to get airborne once again. He knew that even flying a simple circuit would banish the demons before they were able to grow and take hold. As the dust began to settle after the tragedy, Victor took off and flew one solitary circuit of RAF Newchurch. He had lost a fine flight commander, an emerging leader and a good friend. The collision had been a tragic accident that neither pilot was blamed for. That evening 'Bunny' came to visit Victor and after seeing how he was struggling with his injuries, not to mention feeling the need to protect his mental state, ordered him away on four days' leave to rest and recuperate. Flight Lieutenant Patrick 'Dingers' Bell was buried with full military honours on 13 July 1943 at Hawkinge Cemetery.

Somehow, Victor returned on 15 July 1943 'ready' to continue with his duties. The squadron ORB would note 'we are pleased to know that he is feeling much better, although his leg still gives him trouble. We sincerely hope that he will be completely recovered.' On the same day, 19 Squadron led by Wing Commander Bird-Wilson, were in the thick of it as they kept twenty enemy fighters at bay with Flight Lieutenant Wigley, Flying Officer Foster and Sergeant Clydesdale engaging the enemy. Despite all that had occurred in recent weeks, 19 Squadron were once again at the heart of offensive operations with the pressure and intensity about to ramp up to new levels. Just one week after his mid-air collision, Victor would lead the squadron, escorting eighteen Marauders on a diversionary sweep over the Channel.

On 21 July 1943, Victor rang Kim and during the conversation found out that she had fainted whilst on a bus journey the previous day. The pair had been in deep discussion about her service career for weeks and Victor was overjoyed that she had now taken the decision to leave the Women's Auxiliary Air Force. Section Officer Margaret Kimber was pregnant. The couple were thrilled to be expecting their first child and Victor was particularly relieved that she was now away from the demands of service life. He was responsible for the safety of so many people, with the decisions that he made on a daily basis being instrumental to their well-being. For his own peace of mind, he needed to know that Kim and their unborn child would be as safe as they could be under the circumstances. It was a huge relief and huge joy for Victor, and he would end his diary entry simply with the word 'Hooray'.

Over the coming days, he was able to rest and recover from the physical injuries sustained during the mid-air collision and would lead 19 Squadron over occupied Europe on an uneventful 'sweep' on 25 July. The following day the squadron were airborne again with two more missions over Europe. Despite the upheaval on the ground, they were becoming extremely active in the air with Victor taking the weight of the leadership, filling in for the sadly departed 'Dingers'. On a bright, sunny day they flew in a cloudless sky escorting Marauders to Saint-Omer and were pleased to witness accurate bombing that landed on the aerodrome. This raid was followed up by an afternoon 'sweep' flying alongside 132 Squadron. Twenty-four Spitfires roared across the Channel at 'zero' feet before climbing steeply just before the French coast and carrying out a wide sweep around Saint-Omer, to see if there would be any reaction by the Luftwaffe after the morning raid. They flew at 10,000ft and witnessed no enemy aircraft but were harassed by some extremely accurate flak and were grateful to land back at base in one piece at 1655 hours.

Victor had created an extremely cohesive squadron, with a positive atmosphere of unity. It was this environment and the loyal personnel that served within it that enabled him to navigate the constant change and challenge that he confronted on an almost daily basis. One of his staunchest allies during 1943 had been the irrepressible squadron intelligence officer 'Spy' Dilkes. 'Spy' was full of personality and his upbeat demeanour had become a huge tonic to the squadron during the pressures and rigours of front-line fighting. Victor trusted him implicitly and valued his opinion highly, often consulting him on matters concerning 'the boys'. Sadly, at a time when Victor really needed his allies around him, 'Spy' was posted away from 19 Squadron. Devastated at the thought of leaving a squadron that he'd come to love, 'Spy' had pulled as many strings as he could in an attempt to overturn the decision and was 'very distressed' when it had been made clear to him that his services were needed elsewhere. Victor, who was still recovering from the tragic circumstances surrounding the loss of his deputy, was now about to lose yet another close friend. On 27 July 1943, the squadron put their disappointment to one side and visited Ashford in force to bid a memorable farewell to 'Spy'. The squadron ORB would report, rather understatedly, that 'a quiet and quenching quart was quaffed'. In actual fact, a raucous celebration with 'Spy' erupted in the Saracens Head, with Victor spending the latter stages of the evening placating a situation between Pilot Officer Baragwanath and a local policeman who was intent on his arrest. Victor was at his diplomatic best and no further action was taken. At 1030 hours the following morning, the squadron took off to escort Marauders on a raid to Zeebrugge and 'Spy' was seen on the airfield emotionally waving 'his' squadron off for the last time. The squadron ORB would sum up what he meant to 19 Squadron by reporting: 'Spy is off to Group. Their gain is 19 Squadron's loss. He was everybody's friend. So it's goodbye "Spy" and thank you.'

July 1943 ended with a flurry of raids escorting bombers to various locations in occupied France. Victor led from the front as the squadron settled into a new rhythm of operational flying. Each raid was a test for the pilots of 19 Squadron as they existed in a permanent state of concentration and heightened awareness. During the afternoon of 31 July, while escorting Marauders, the formation was attacked by twelve determined enemy aircraft. Victor's situational awareness in the air allowed him to read what was developing and he instructed his squadron to break and engage the enemy. Yet another huge dogfight took place in the skies above France, with Flying Officer Mills and Sergeant Wass able to damage multiple machines. Flying Officer Mills would find himself in the heart of the scrap but even when trapped between two Fw 190s he was able to hold his own and return,

Pilot Officer Peter Wass.

dangerously low on fuel, back to England. It was a turbulent end to an extremely turbulent month for the squadron, and for Victor. Despite everything that had taken place, he was able to carry on with the task of leading the squadron because of the solidarity that he felt among his men. Their morale held firm among constant change and it had an extremely galvanising effect on him. He had complete support from 'the boys' and his mid-air collision would spark a flurry of letters from well-wishers, including ground crews, praising his quick thinking and wishing him well. It was also a time when the hierarchy of 122 Wing let their actions do the talking with many visits from 'Bunny' and 'Birdy' that led to the usual evenings in the pub. He could feel this solidarity and was extremely grateful for it.

Almost as a tonic to the previous month's endeavours, August 1943 started in high spirits. High winds had led to the pilots being released from flying duties for twenty-four hours and 19 Squadron gratefully took the opportunity to head into Ashford to celebrate the

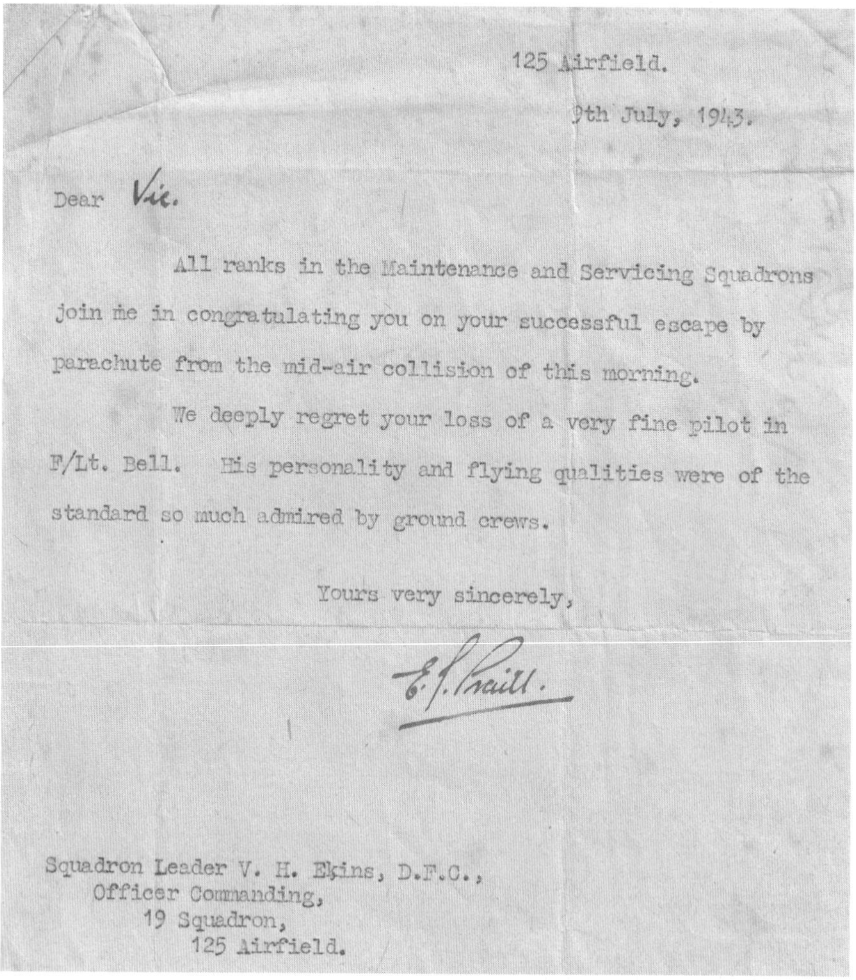

125 Airfield.

9th July, 1943.

Dear Vic,

All ranks in the Maintenance and Servicing Squadrons join me in congratulating you on your successful escape by parachute from the mid-air collision of this morning.

We deeply regret your loss of a very fine pilot in F/Lt. Bell. His personality and flying qualities were of the standard so much admired by ground crews.

Yours very sincerely,

E. J. Praill.

Squadron Leader V. H. Ekins, D.F.C.,
    Officer Commanding,
      19 Squadron,
        125 Airfield.

A letter received from relieved members of 19 Squadron ground crew congratulating Victor for his 'successful escape' after the mid air collision with 'Dingers' Bell on 9 July 1943.

twenty-first birthday of Flying Officer Johnnie 'Stretch' Foster. The ORB would summarise the evening by saying:

> 'A tour of the locals was headed by Johnnie himself and finally ended in The Saracens Head, where 23 merry types forced an entrance to an already crowded lounge. On the

Flying Officer Johnnie 'Stretch' Foster.

The pilots of 19 Squadron endured over 6 months of living under 'the dreaded canvas'.

Flying Officer Ian Mundy.

return to camp Johnnie was given a friendly "doing over"
as an initiation to his reaching manhood.'

It's easy to forget given the demands and pressure exerted while
airborne that these were just young men trying to enjoy life. To
further bolster these high spirits, the squadron then welcomed
Flight Lieutenant 'Tommy' Drinkwater to their ranks as the new
commander of 'B' Flight. He was an outstanding leader and skilful
fighter pilot who would fit into the squadron seamlessly after serving
234 Squadron with distinction. He had arrived just in time for yet
another squadron move but this time it coincided with some great
news: they were about to be re-equipped with the Spitfire IX. This
new mark was absolutely adored by those who flew it. It maintained
its trademark balance and manoeuvrability but was vastly improved
with heavier armament, a more powerful engine and a higher ceiling
of operations. The Focke-Wulf Fw 190 had been ruling the skies
above Europe but the Spitfire IX was turning the tables back in favour
of Fighter Command and now 19 Squadron would experience this

Squadron Leader Ekins sits centre of shot with the 'boys' from 19 Squadron.

shift first hand. Now based at 122 Airfield Kingsnorth, the pilots eagerly gathered around Wing Commander Bird-Wilson, who gave them all the latest 'gen' on their new steed. They enjoyed two days of acclimatisation and on 22 August were on the offensive once again in an extremely buoyant mood.

Over the next five days, Victor would lead 19 Squadron on raids over occupied Europe on no fewer than seven occasions. The pride he felt at being at the front of this loyal and dedicated group of warriors was undeniable. He cared deeply for the safety and progression of each and every one of them. Being at the helm of a front-line squadron was an all-consuming role but, typically, Victor gave absolutely everything he had into making it the best it could be. Standards were high and discipline was essential but among these necessities

Squadron Leader Victor Ekins DFC.

were loyalty, friendship and humour. The biggest issue that Victor faced was the constant change the squadron experienced with regard to finding a base that it could call home but even this hardship was endured as one. Squadron Leader Victor Ekins DFC was leading a front-line fighter squadron that flew the most advanced Spitfire in service, which found itself at the forefront of taking the fight to Germany by tactically identifying and attacking targets of vital importance for the planned invasion of Europe. The inexperienced sergeant pilot who had endured the baptism of fire during the early weeks of the Battle of Britain had come a long way.

It was becoming more regular for the squadron to be escorting the American Flying Fortress bombers by day and, due to their new aircraft, they began to operate at vastly higher altitudes. On 23 August, the squadron were flying at 25,000ft when the oxygen pipe came off Victor's face mask and he passed out. His Spitfire fell a full 10,000ft, spinning wildly out of control, before he eventually regained consciousness and groggily pulled the aircraft out of its dive. He returned back to base a little shaken but was able to spend an enjoyable evening with 'Bunny', in the company of Wing Commander 'Johnnie' Johnson and Group Captain 'Woody' Woodhall for what he described as a 'good night'. His overriding feeling of this first week in their new aircraft was the extreme cold that the squadron endured as they flew ever higher but he managed to acquire some electrically heated gloves that seemed to ease the discomfort. They encountered heavy flak on almost every raid, with the formation jumping and rocking among the explosions but enemy aircraft were few and far between. This proved to be a huge frustration for the pilots of 19 Squadron, who were more determined than ever to achieve their next aerial victory – they had money riding on it.

For weeks now, a sweepstake had existed on who would be the pilot to shoot down 19 Squadron's '100th Hun'. They had been tantalisingly stuck on ninety-nine victories for some time and despite numerous combats with the enemy had been unable to confirm the all-important success. With the introduction of Flight Lieutenant Drinkwater, the squadron now had a very experienced and determined feel indeed. Victor would lead from the front, with Drinkwater and Wigley as his flight commanders. They then had a plethora of experienced and motivated flying officers, pilot officers and sergeants with whom to make up their respective flights. Add to this the fact that they now flew the most up to date and modern mark of Spitfire in front-line service and it's fair to say that a new offensive zeal swept throughout the squadron, not to mention the prestige of going down in the squadron's history books as being the pilot to claim the all-important victory. During the first fifteen days of September 1943, the squadron flew on missions over occupied Europe a staggering nineteen times. For the vast majority of these flights Victor would lead 'the boys' as they escorted bombers or carried out offensive 'sweeps' trying to lure the Luftwaffe into the fight. On 3 September Sergeant Ritchie developed trouble with his engine, which shut down altogether as the squadron recrossed the French coast after a raid. Flying Officer Ross was flying alongside him when at 4,000ft he witnessed the Spitfire beginning to lose height rapidly. Sergeant Ritchie was left with no choice but to take to his parachute and was seen to be almost immediately picked up by German Air Sea Rescue. It was a strange mix of emotions for the squadron, who were both relieved with the fact that he was safe but also bitterly disappointed to lose a member of the squadron who would now sit out the rest of the war as a PoW.

On 6 September 1943 the squadron were up at dawn and airborne by 0650 hours escorting seventy-two Marauders on a raid to Rouen. They landed at 0820 hours but were needed for another operation shortly after as they took off to cover the withdrawal of Flying Fortresses that had bombed Stuttgart. After a brief pause, where Victor managed to steal an hour's sleep, they were airborne again later in the afternoon acting as high cover for Marauders. Flying at 25,000ft, they sighted many enemy machines but frustratingly none engaged and they recrossed the coast without incident. Victor would simply write in his diary '1000 bombers over France and Germany in daylight.' On their way home, the squadron then lowered to sea level in response to a

An exhausted Victor takes a moment's rest in between offensive operations.

request to search for Flying Fortress crews who had been lost in an earlier raid and come down in 'the drink'. They carried out an air sea rescue search and were able to successfully locate three dinghies full of very grateful American airmen, plotting their position and waiting for motor launches to come and rescue them. On their way home they saw two partially floating Flying Fortresses that had ditched into the sea but no crew could be seen. The squadron landed back at base at 1900 hours and after a quick meal and freshen up headed out in force to attend a local concert before returning to the mess, now a bell tent, to drink and laugh until almost midnight. After a restless night's sleep in their makeshift accommodation, they then rose at dawn and were airborne by 0800 hours acting as high cover for eighty Flying Fortresses bombing Watten Wood. And so it continued. This was the relentless routine that 19 Squadron were now committed to and the fact of the matter was that they were operating from what was effectively a campsite.

The pace of operations didn't let up as time and again 19 Squadron operated deep over enemy territory. On 9 September Victor chased two 109s 'down to the deck' after they had threatened to attack the bomber formation but was unable to get close enough to attack. As the month developed, so too did the Luftwaffe's desire to get into the fight as more and more enemy machines tried to disrupt the bomber formations. On 16 September Pilot Officer Baragwanath went close as he fired several shots at a Fw 190, along with Flying Officer Page and Sergeant Biggs. On 21 September Flight Lieutenant Wigley managed to get on the tail of a Fw 190 and, in an intense dogfight, expended all of his ammunition at the enemy machine but was unable to confirm the result of the attack as it dived steeply away. No. 19 Squadron were well and truly in the groove of offensive operations and extremely motivated to protect the bomber force at all costs but as the end of September approached, so too did the autumnal weather conditions. The heavens opened and flying time started to become a little more restricted, with multiple raids being cancelled at the last minute. On 29 September, the squadron packed up their tents for the last time as they were asked to negotiate yet another move, this time to RAF Weston Zoyland. This came as a huge relief to one and all as it contained quarters that could sleep all of the personnel. The squadron ORB would comment: 'It was agreed that life on a static station was very much the 'form' after 6 months on the airfield. Thankfully, the camping days are over.' Victor had been leading 19 Squadron for ten months and six of those had been while sleeping on a camp bed, living among the most basic of conditions. He was constantly concerned about his squadron and was forced to consider their most basic needs of warmth, shelter and decent food on a regular basis. This primitive living, added to the constant upheaval, was piled onto the already demanding workload of a squadron leader operating on the offensive. Victor carried this load with the dignity and stoicism that he'd learned during his boarding school days but he couldn't deny the feeling that his focus also lay elsewhere. Kim and their unborn baby were also at the forefront of his mind and after over three years of front-line service the conversation had arisen as to how long he would go on for. For now though, he had a job to do.

At RAF Weston Zoyland the indifferent weather conditions continued with the squadron getting airborne infrequently to practise dogfighting and carry out dummy attacks on a drogue. They weren't able to fly any operational sorties before they were moved on once again, this time to RAF Gatwick on 16 October 1943. They had known in advance that this latest posting would be temporary as a permanent home had been identified, with the move being planned for the near future. Thankfully, a window of good weather opened up and offensive operations resumed the following day, which culminated in Victor being given the honour of leading 122 Wing on a raid to Beauvais aerodrome on 24 October 1943. The formation of three fighter squadrons flying alongside seventy-two Marauders formed up 20 miles north of Dieppe and flew at 23,000ft towards their target. Maintaining top cover, the raid went according to plan with no resistance from either enemy aircraft or flak defences and the wing leader flying led all aircraft home safely, landing at 1310 hours. It would prove to be the last operational flight of the month as bad weather set in yet again, with Victor commenting 'clampers ho'. All the pilots breathed a huge sigh of relief when it was confirmed that their latest base, now RAF Gravesend, would be their permanent home. It contained all of the facilities that a front-line fighter squadron required and was perfectly situated for a good night out, being so close to London. Victor had planned, prepared and executed a staggering eleven squadron moves in just ten months. The logistical demand on him had been huge and he was exceedingly grateful to be suitably accommodated on an established airfield. No. 19 Squadron had essentially led a nomadic existence since the start of 1943 and were held together by the guidance and commitment of their squadron leader. Now, they could truly focus on the task in hand, the '100th Hun'.

As autumn turned to winter, the Second Tactical Air Force was blessed with a window of fair weather that allowed them to take the attack to Germany once again. On 3 November 1943 Victor led the squadron as they acted as high cover protecting Marauders bombing Saint-André-de-l'Eure aerodrome and then later the same day flew with the squadron as they protected bombers that were attacking Schiphol aerodrome in Amsterdam. It was the start of an extremely active period of flying as they went on to complete ten escort missions within the first eleven days of the month. Enemy aircraft were present more often than not but they wouldn't engage the formation, or when they did, it would often be another squadron in position to counter the attack.

The 11 November 1943 was a fine and clear autumn day, with the squadron once again called into action. They were tasked with carrying out a fighter sweep in the Saint-Pol area as a diversion for bombing that was going to take place on construction works on the Cherbourg peninsula. They had been over France for about thirty minutes when 122 Squadron were attacked by sixteen Fw 190s.

No. 19 Squadron immediately turned towards them and, as they approached, a single enemy machine broke away and began to dive down. Flight Lieutenant 'Tommy' Drinkwater reacted in an instant and headed down after it, firing as he went. The pair plunged into a steep dive that took them down from 18,000ft to just 1,000ft, with Flight Lieutenant Drinkwater firing a number of bursts that he could clearly see hitting the mark. After one last determined attack, the Fw 190 gave in under the pressure and crash-landed in a field, becoming the squadron's 100th confirmed aerial victory. When Flight Lieutenant Drinkwater landed, he was treated to a hero's reception and that evening 'the boys' headed out in force to celebrate this momentous occasion at the Ship Inn. Everyone was in incredibly high spirits, which only got higher when 'Spy' Dilkes walked through the door to join the party. He was 19 Squadron through and through and wouldn't have missed this for the world. For all that they had given to the fight for freedom during 1943, achieving the squadron's 100th victory was the least that they deserved and Victor revelled in the atmosphere and brotherhood of life with 19 Squadron. The boisterous atmosphere, the smoke-filled rooms and the free-flowing beers enjoyed with his 'boys' would leave an indelible mark in Victor's heart. He would never forget nights like this.

As 1943 began to draw to a close, the Second Tactical Air Force began a serious shake-up of personnel in preparation for the invasion of Europe, which they knew would take place the following year. On 26 November Wing Commander Bird-Wilson left 122 Wing and Victor took the opportunity to speak with his old friend 'Bunny' Currant about his own position. Other than a six-month break away from operations, Victor had been fighting on the front line since 2 August 1940 and he knew deep down that it was time. He had given everything of himself once again, under extremely challenging circumstances, and was immensely proud of the current shape that his squadron was in. Victor was always there to do his duty but, in his heart of hearts, he recognised the fact that 1944 would almost certainly see the invasion of occupied Europe and the need for drive, energy, and an unadulterated offensive spirit. There was also the fact that in six weeks' time he would also be at the start of another exciting chapter in his life: fatherhood. He and 'Bunny' spoke at length and it was agreed that the time was right to leave his beloved 19 Squadron and put his experience to good use elsewhere in the Royal Air Force. He had led 'the boys' with complete dedication for just over a year and was determined to tie up a few loose ends before his departure, namely organising the official celebratory party for the squadron's '100th Hun'.

On 1 December, Victor led 19 Squadron as they met 250 Flying Fortresses, which were on the return leg of a mission that had seen them bombing deep into Germany. It was a gruelling flight that lasted over two hours, with Victor having to split the squadron into sections as they protected various bombers that had been damaged during the raid and were struggling to get back to base. Three days later he was airborne once again leading a fighter sweep over Lille. On 5 December he would lead the squadron for the final time as they carried out another fighter sweep, this time over Cambrai. Although he didn't know it at the time, it would prove to be his last operational sortie of the war. The next day saw an extreme change in the weather as a thick fog descended on London, with these unfavourable flying conditions lasting for two weeks. Victor took the opportunity to send out invitations and plan the forthcoming celebrations as 19 Squadron looked ahead to a well-deserved end of year 'party and dance'.

On 18 December 1943 the squadron gathered in force at 23 Knightsbridge for the official '100th Hun' celebration. The party began at 2000 hours and would go on into the early hours as Victor soaked up the atmosphere and friendship with 'the boys'. The hero of the moment, Flight Lieutenant Drinkwater, was given the honour of cutting the cake at the gathering, which included many special guests one of whom was Victor's sister, Cynthia, and they danced into the night. He would write in his diary 'marvellous show, everything

19 (FIGHTER) SQUADRON ROYAL AIR FORCE
❖
The Commanding Officer
(Squadron Leader V. H. Ekins, D.F.C.)
and Members of 19 Squadron
request the pleasure of the company of

to a Party and Dance to be held at
No. 23 KNIGHTSBRIDGE, LONDON,
to celebrate their Hundredth Victory.
SATURDAY, 18th DECEMBER, 1943, 8 till 2.

R.S.V.P. to—
C.O. 19 Squadron,   BUFFET
Gravesend.   Dress Optional

The invitation sent out for the '100th Hun' celebration on 18 December 1943.

Flight Lieutenant Drinkwater cuts the cake in recognition of his success.

grand' as he spent time with each member of the squadron, enjoying their company for what was to become Victor's unofficial farewell to 19 Squadron. On 22 December, it was with mixed feelings that he noted 'self definitely posted, no more flying for me' in his diary, before finally leaving the boys on 27 December 1943. The whole squadron gathered in dispersal to say farewell to their commanding officer and were incredibly sorry to see him go. There was an overriding feeling of gratitude, affection and appreciation for the man who had led them into battle. He had defended them both in the air and on the ground, showing complete devotion to his men during a year that they would never forget. Squadron Leader Victor Ekins DFC had encouraged, challenged, guided, protected and inspired the pilots who had served under him and his time with 19 Squadron would forever hold a special place in his heart. His positive influence is best summed up in a letter written by squadron member S.E. Loughlan:

> It is that very habit of recognising always the slightest kindness done to yourself and placing on record that recognition, that makes everyone so happy to do anything for you – that service, small service enough, was gladly rendered by both Dilkes and myself, and will be rendered again and again to you by all kinds of people as you go through life, as long as you retain and I hope and see no reason to believe that you will not always retain your sunny, happy and kindly disposition. I have often thought how much you and Farmer Lawson had in common and how much you would have liked one another. He was like yourself, an honest, upright English Gentleman with no tricks in his dealings.

16

Duty Calls

As was expected of every person during war, duty and service had always been Victor's priority but he was exceedingly glad to put service life to one side for a short time and take some leave to be with Kim at Torquay. They celebrated the New Year together but the following night Kim slept very badly and, after consulting the family doctor, she was taken to Bovey Tracey Hospital as a precaution. Typically, as Kim and Victor prepared themselves for the imminent arrival of their first child, he received a message requesting his attendance at Fighter Command HQ 'at once'. The timing of the request couldn't have been any worse but Victor had no choice but to leave Kim with the support of her family and travel to London, catching a train from Paignton. His first thought on arrival was to explain the situation and 'fix some leave', which was duly granted but he first had to have a meeting to confirm his new posting as an instructor at 53 Operational Training Unit at Kirton in Lindsey. On 4 January 1944, Kim gave birth to a healthy baby boy, who the couple decided to name Anthony, after Victor's dear and departed friend, Anthony Palmer-Tomkinson. He was thrilled to hear the news, commenting 'so pleased, Kim and Son are ok. Very thrilled and very excited', and immediately caught a train back to Torquay. On 6 January he held Anthony for the first time and would note 'Both wonderful. Kim looks marvellous.' For the next twelve days the Ekins family, as they had now become, enjoyed some precious time together and Victor revelled in his new role. The transience of his wartime existence had meant that only ten days previously he had been a squadron leader in charge of a front-line fighter squadron. Now, he was an instructor and an extremely proud father. On 18 January 1944, it was heart-breaking to leave his family behind but duty called and he made his way north to Kirton in Lindsey to start the latest chapter in his service career.

After the nomadic existence that Victor had experienced during the majority of his time commanding 19 Squadron, life at Kirton in Lindsey proved to be a welcome tonic. His new role as the commanding officer of an advanced training squadron would see him working with the next batch of front-line fighter pilots as they completed the final stage of their training. They were by now capable airmen but this advanced stage had been designed to equip them with the tools needed to serve the RAF operationally and in combat. Victor had, of course, been through this stage before but his wartime experiences had led him to believe that his focus should not solely be on their performance in the air. In his view, each airman should understand and be able to integrate into the 'ways of the squadron' before they were posted. He would give each course that he taught at 53 OTU a lecture on 'squadron life' and would actively promote a spirit of oneness and camaraderie with the recruits. He had felt the solidarity and strength of squadron life, and used his experience to give these eager airmen a telling insight into this unique world. As was always the way with Victor, high standards and discipline in the air were absolute non-negotiables.

The trainees themselves were a mix of diverse young men who had all joined the RAF during what would become the latter stages of the war. They could see the progress that was being made by the Allies and were desperate not to miss out on the action. As a result, Victor would have to contend with groups of overconfident, impatient and at times boisterous young men who were itching to get into the fight. His patient and experienced manner made him perfect for the job. Victor was able to implement many of the routines of a front-line squadron, where each member would be expected to

Victor sits centre of the front row, as an instructor at 53 OTU at Kirton in Lindsey.

make their own contribution. He would guide them both on the ground and in the air with a firm but fair attitude and a genuine desire to extract the very best from each of them. While airborne, the recruits were put through their paces with hours spent practising formation flying and mock dogfighting. One of the exercises that Victor prioritised would see the squadron flying in formation as he took the role of lone attacker and 'bounced' the recruits as he'd seen the Luftwaffe do countless times in the past. This would, of course, take them completely by surprise, with him commenting 'bounced the formation. Chaps not very good'. Still, far better to make the mistakes and learn those lessons under Victor's experienced tutelage. They would be prone to heavy landings, landing with wheels up, taxiing collisions and a general naivety in the air that was almost a rite of passage for every airman who passed through Royal Air Force training.

As the weeks turned into months, Victor also became extremely grateful for the stability that came with this new career path. He forged an extremely close bond with Group Captain John Hawtrey and the rest of the instructors at 53 OTU, who would regularly socialise together. They would also enjoy a range of activities in the evenings such as games of squash, badminton, snooker and table tennis. For Victor, the ability to be able to put down some roots also had a quite literal meaning as he immersed himself

Group Captain John Hawtrey and Victor.

into a regular routine of gardening and growing vegetables. It was a welcome and long overdue reconnection with nature that extended as far as introducing beehives to Kirton in Lindsey. He was running things 'his' way without the constant expectation of being uprooted that had so often been the case during his time with 19 Squadron. As 1944 passed, Victor threw himself into life as an instructor but would be in almost constant contact with Kim and would visit his beloved family at any given opportunity.

One huge advantage to his time at Kirton in Lindsey was the fact that he was still able to get airborne and take to the skies in a Spitfire. In actual fact, Victor would 'claim' a specific aircraft of his own that would become his personal steed for the majority of 1944. Spitfire P8591 had been through the wars and had a host of mechanical faults that Victor experienced as early as 29 January 1944, with a faulty RT.

It was constantly being grounded and failing air tests but he never once gave up on 'his' machine. The thing that made this particular aircraft special to Victor was the fact that his name was emblazoned down the side of it. The code letters VI*C were clear for everyone to see and he affectionately referred to it in his diary as 'Vic'. Royal Air Force protocol stated that a wing commander flying could have his initials painted on the side of his aircraft for ease of identification but never an abbreviated name. The squadron codes VI*C belonged to 169 Squadron but they never operated Spitfires so the aircraft was either an anomaly or Victor himself had the letters painted on the side. Given his predisposition to 'bounce' the recruits while they were flying in formation, then I would suggest that a quick identification was of the utmost importance. Either way, Victor Ekins was one of the few pilots, if not the only member of the Royal Air Force, to have his name painted down the side of his own personal Spitfire during the Second World War.

Throughout the whole of 1944, Victor would comment with interest on the events that were taking place around the world and, on 6 June he would emblazon in red pencil the words 'INVASION OF FRANCE'. It was a huge turning point for the Allies as they fought hard to regain a foot hold in Nazi-occupied Europe and begin the slow advance forward towards liberation. The following month he would comment 'Trouble in Germany. Hitler nearly killed' and in August 1944 he would jubilantly write 'PARIS LIBERATED'. He would at times experience moments of feeling out of the loop as he kept up to date with news of 19 Squadron, who were based in France and supporting the advance, but tried to concentrate on the task in hand and gave his all to nurturing the next crop of front-line pilots. It was during the summer months that he notched up another huge landmark as a pilot flying for the Royal Air Force: over 1,000 hours of flight experience.

Victor had the capability to make each airman that passed through 53 OTU feel like they were part of something special. This also included the effort that was put into their passing out ceremony at

Above and below: Victor standing next to 'his' Spitfire P8591.

the end of their course. In a smoke-filled room, he would hush the boisterous atmosphere and address the current course members, who listened intently with pints of beer in hand. An example of one of his parting gestures can be seen in the following poem that was written and recited for the members of No. 46 Course:

I shall sing you a song about chaps in the mess
They work at this unit or try, I confess
But day by day they do work with a song and a smile
And at night you see letch written over each dial
Also Uncle J.

The first in the list is the G/C himself
He's of manageable age but is still on the shelf
He spent years out in India among the heat and the flies
Now there'll be Kirton engraved on his heart when he
dies
Poor Uncle.

Winco H West is the chief man in training
He's always doing air tests to see if it's raining
His new Spitty 5 is cropped and a sorter
In the bar he'll be heard ordering whiskey and water
With Uncle

Our stores branch is run by a bonny Scot, Jock
He's a solicitor by trade and helps chaps in the dock
He handles his job with the greatest of ease
And delights to make use of his 674B's
To Uncle

Now there's Gibson the plumber, a man of repute
He looks after the bar and so can buy a new suit

DUTY CALLS

If you want anything done he's the man to contact
But he drinks like a fish as a matter of fact
With Uncle

Now Wilson the gas man with fire engines too
By cranking his motors breaks his wrist into two
He finds it most awkward not being able to write
And when told there's a fire remarks "keep it alight"
For Uncle

Now Hunter the sports king is frightfully fit
His body is lovely when in a PT kit
He's out on the razzle most nights we are told
But let us hear more of his story unfold
To Uncle

Our medical man is named Doctor Stone
He has cures for every disease ever known
He loves doing work and carrying out tests
On how to make WAAFS develop their breasts
For Uncle

Each station is blessed with a S/Ldr 'A'
At this place his name is appropriately Way
But way in or way out doesn't matter a hoot
If he doesn't like Hokers he just gives them the boot
For Uncle

There's Browning an int bloke, a most learned type
He's got all the gen about news and the like
What he doesn't know surely isn't worth knowing
You read it and don't know if you're coming or going
To Uncle

Our instructors just now are as busy as hell
They work half the day and like drinking as well
They long to return to their squadrons in France
And hope that the French girls will give them a chance
Also Uncle

Now 46 Course are about to depart
We've enjoyed their company right from the start
We wish them good luck and good hunting as well
And trust they'll send hundreds of Huns into Hell
For Uncle

After almost a year of nurturing and developing the next crop of fighter pilots, Victor was informed that he would be moving on once more, this time to 12 Group HQ at RAF Watnall as a staff officer. On 12 December he packed up his belongings and 'said goodbye to the chaps and GC'. The 'GC' mentioned was his now close friend Group Captain John Hawtrey, who would later sum up Victor's time as an instructor with the following letter:

It is to say how sorry I was to lose you and to thank you for all you did for me and for 53 OTU. And of course, as is the way of the world, it is only when you have gone and all those things which have gone right for so long, start going wrong, that one realises the extent of your work and your influence and your ability to co-operate and to get things done.

Well Vic, you made Kirton and 53 OTU because you made the last phase like a proper squadron and of course you made my time here.

I shall hope to see you frequently till the end of my life.

Yours ever

John Hawtrey (G/C)'

Victor, Kim and Anthony saw in their first new year together under the dark clouds of war but there was a feeling that the end might be near. The whole world watched on at the start of 1945 as the Allied advance swept through Europe, and Russia made huge gains from the East. Life at 12 Group was engaging but quite challenging for Victor as he'd only ever known a heavy workload that he gladly undertook among an atmosphere of drive and purpose. As the end of the war came into sight he struggled to adjust to the slower pace and the feeling of redundancy went completely against the grain. Despite these challenges, his standards never slipped and he completed what was asked of him to the highest of his ability. As the months passed it became clear that an Allied victory was all but certain. Kim had been battling a feeling of isolation as she experienced the early stages of parenthood without the support of Victor and that only made his desire to be with his family greater. She was a free-spirited and extremely independent woman, and the isolation that she felt was beginning to take its toll. Victor would regularly write of how he 'missed' his family and 'wished' he could be with them but it was a time when they had to be patient.

On 7 May 1945, Victor gratefully took some leave to be with Kim and Anthony among a flurry of rumours that the war was about to end and that evening he would write the unforgettable words 'WAR WITH GERMANY OVER'. The following day the Ekins family gathered around the radio at 1500 hours to listen to Winston Churchill's broadcast and spent a 'wonderful day' together celebrating VE Day. It was a huge relief for a couple that had given so much, for so many years, in pursuit of this moment. A moment where Europe was once again free from the tyranny of an oppressive regime. As with so many others, they had given everything of themselves and selflessly put their young lives on pause for a cause that was worthy of fighting for. It was time to move on with their lives and, for Kim and Victor, that meant finding a home for their family and finally being with one another during times of peace.

Kim with son, Anthony Ekins.

On 25 August 1945 Victor took to the skies for the last time, fittingly flying a Supermarine Spitfire. He flew from RAF Hucknall to the closest base to his home town, RAF Graveley. The man who piloted that aircraft was almost unrecognisable from the young sergeant pilot who completed his training just in time to be thrust into the middle of the Battle of Britain five years earlier. At 31 years old, an accomplished squadron leader wearing the much-coveted DFC ribbon on his chest now held the controls of the Spitfire and was completely at one with this incredible machine. His flying ability was totally natural as a mere thought would seamlessly transmit through his body and then onto the control column of his aircraft as it responded to his every command. As he glanced out of the cockpit, he couldn't help but stare at the cannon situated in the wing of his aircraft. The tense yet exhilarating memories of aerial combat as these now silent cannon that had once roared were still at the very forefront of his mind. He would never forget. The loss of dear friends whose fresh-faced smiles still entered his mind with a pang of nostalgia would never leave him. As RAF Graveley came into sight, Victor lowered his undercarriage, entered the circuit and slipped off some excess height before selecting flaps down, as he'd done so countless times before. His Spitfire landed gracefully on the airfield and he taxied across to dispersal, cut the engine and watched the propeller come to a standstill. His service was done.

As the dust settled and the world began to heal after enduring a conflict that had stolen 60 million lives, Victor was grateful to be finally demobilised on 29 September 1945. The Ekins family moved back to St Neots and Victor was able to do his duty to his father and rejoin the family business that he'd left almost ten years earlier. Sydney Ekins had been feeling the strain of the increased workload that the war had placed on him and his advancing years forced him to accept that he needed help. Victor began to adore his work and was at his happiest either at the agricultural auction or at home with his family. He found himself at the heart of his community and couldn't walk down the high street of his home town without people knowing who he was and stopping to say hello. On 26 January 1948 the Ekins family became joyfully complete with the birth of their second son, Paul.

Victor would rarely, if ever, talk about the war but his experiences never left him. He would often be heard by his family in the middle of the night, gripped in the midst of a nightmare trying to escape a burning aircraft. The intensity of the moment would be soothed by his beloved Kim as she reassured her husband that all was well. Kim understood, for their love had somehow blossomed in a world torn apart by war. In a world where Victor had served with a front-line fighter squadron and duelled with his foe in a life-or-death battle for twenty-one continuous months. In a world where both had been gripped with fear as bombs had rained down all around them. Victor had fallen 'head over heels' in love with Kim the moment that they had met at RAF Kenley and he would carry on loving her deeply until his dying day.

During the summer of 1949, Anthony Ekins would recall standing beside his father on the bridge at St Neots, overlooking the River Ouse. Victor hadn't exactly left his service life empty handed and his sons would have fond memories of flying helmets, goggles, gloves and boots hanging in the family home. Another item that had accompanied Victor into life on civvy street was his service revolver. He had recently been asked to be on the finishing line of a race at the local regatta and had taken the opportunity to dust off his gun and end proceedings with a bang. Kim hadn't been impressed and, after a discussion between the two, it was decided that it was time to part with it. The symbolism of the moment that followed should never be forgotten. There he stood in his home town, with his son by his side, who had been named after a dear and departed friend lost during the war. In his hand he held an instrument of war that had accompanied him on countless missions flying over occupied Europe. Victor drew back his arm and threw the revolver as far as he could, watching it plunge into the river below.

Kim and Victor would go on to spend a long and happy life together.

Remembering Victor

What a privilege it has been immersing myself in the world of Victor Ekins. The process of researching his story has taken over three years and during this time we have shared some incredibly special moments. The project has had an energy behind it that has silently pushed us forward and guided us towards unearthing some untold treasures from the past. As a team, we feel that these moments deserve a place in this book and it's our pleasure to share the unforgettable journey that we have been on remembering Victor.

Epilogue

On the day that I first met Anthony Ekins he not only showed me Victor's collection but gave me permission to take it home and begin to understand its contents. When I talk about the trust that I have felt from the Ekins family it literally began on day one. After taking the collection from Anthony, I immediately went to my parents' house and this is the picture that we took after we'd laid it all out. My mum and I were absolutely speechless.

As a team, we began to discuss how we could commemorate Victor's achievements and celebrate a local hero whose modesty had kept his story untold for over 80 years. The picture is of Anthony and I after we'd taken delivery of the blue plaque that was soon to be unveiled on 28 New Street, St Neots.

The blue plaque was unveiled on 15th September (Battle of Britain day) 2020.
Victor was born in the back bedroom of 28 New Street on 16th April 1914.

Shortly after the blue plaque was unveiled, we collaborated with St Neots Museum and exhibited Victor's collection to the public. This picture was taken on the day and shows myself and my mum, Chris Duker. Without her involvement this project just couldn't have happened. She spent three months transcribing over 80,000 words from five years' worth of diaries.

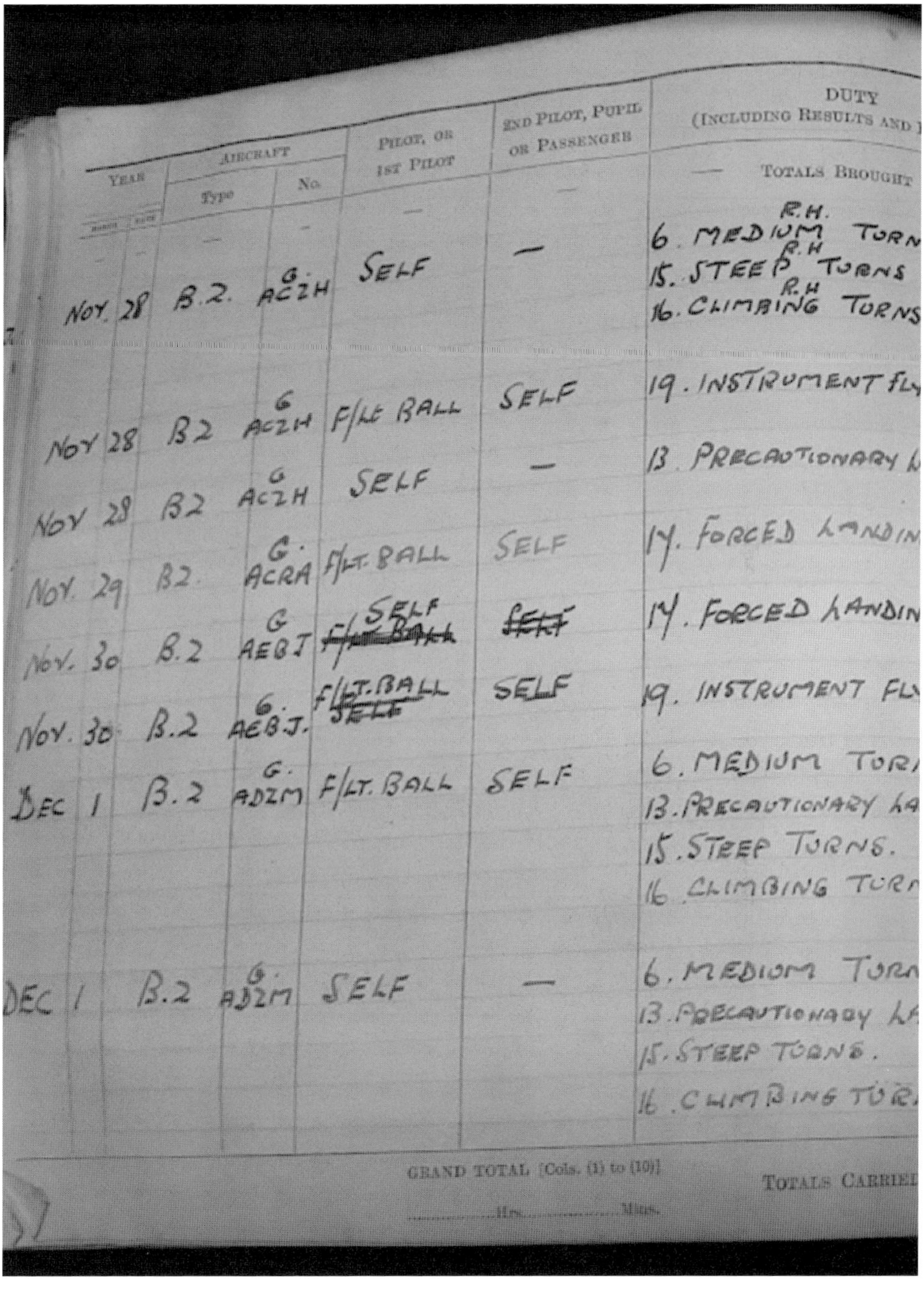

YEAR		AIRCRAFT		PILOT, OR 1ST PILOT	2ND PILOT, PUPIL OR PASSENGER	DUTY (INCLUDING RESULTS AND
		Type	No.			TOTALS BROUGHT
		—	—	—	—	
NOV. 28		B.2.	G. ACZH	SELF	—	6. MEDIUM TURN R.H. 15. STEEP TURNS R.H. 16. CLIMBING TURNS R.H
NOV 28		B2	G. ACZH	F/Lt BALL	SELF	19. INSTRUMENT FLY
NOV 28		B2	G. ACZH	SELF	—	13. PRECAUTIONARY L
NOV. 29		B2.	G. ACRA	F/LT. BALL	SELF	14. FORCED LANDIN
NOV. 30		B.2	G. AEBJ	~~F/~~ SELF ~~Lt BALL~~	~~SELF~~	14. FORCED LANDIN
NOV. 30		B.2	G. AEBJ.	F/LT.BALL ~~SELF~~	SELF	19. INSTRUMENT FLY
DEC 1		B.2	G. ADZM	F/LT. BALL	SELF	6. MEDIUM TUR 13. PRECAUTIONARY LA 15. STEEP TURNS. 16 CLIMBING TURN
DEC 1		B.2	G. ADZM	SELF	—	6. MEDIUM TUR 13. PRECAUTIONARY LA 15. STEEP TURNS. 16. CLIMBING TUR

GRAND TOTAL [Cols. (1) to (10)]

.... Hrs. .... Mins.

TOTALS CARRIED

Victor's logbook shows that during his training he flew the Blackburn B2 aircraft. On 30th November 1939 he practised forced landings and instrument flying in G-AEBJ.

215

Being a rare aircraft, we were able to locate the very same Blackburn B2, now displayed as part of the Shuttleworth Collection. With the help of Dominic Ward, Anthony and Paul Ekins were able to get up close and personal with G-AEBJ

Anthony Ekins sits in the cockpit of G-AEBJ.

Paul Ekins sits in the cockpit of G-AEBJ.

Paul Ekins sits at his piano and plays the same music that Victor so often played during his war years. To make this emotional moment even more special, he played from Victor's original song sheets.

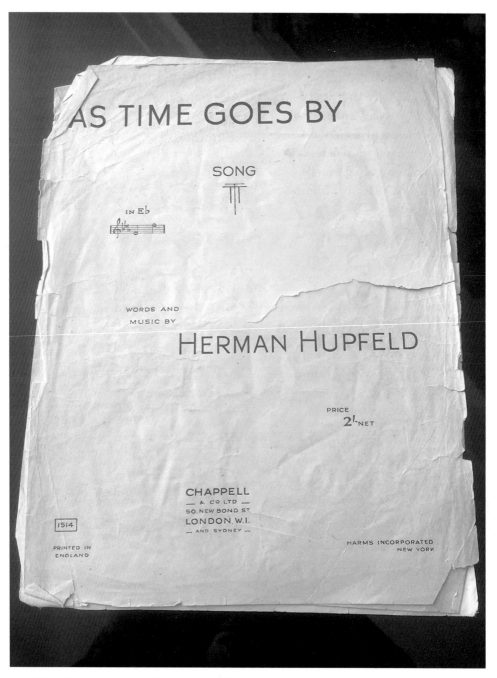

Victor's wartime song sheet of 'As Time Goes By'.

The Ekins family decided that the spiritual home for Victor's collection was the Kent Battle of Britain Museum Trust at Hawkinge. This picture was taken during the handover as we talked with Dave Brocklehurst MBE, the chairman of the museum.

Above left: This picture of Victor was taken whilst he was a squadron leader with 19 Squadron. The chain of his dog tag can be seen under his battle dress, next to his tie.

Above right: Through my work with the Tally Ho Project CIC, we were able to deliver a talk about the Battle of Britain to the students of Surbiton High Prep school. What made this day particularly special was the fact that Victor's Great Grandson, Dan Pullinger was in attendance. He was able to dress up as a fighter pilot and also wear the same dog tag that Victor had worn during his wartime years (seen hanging around his neck in the photo).

Dan Pullinger proudly standing in front of a picture of his
Great Grandfather.

Index